UNFLINCHING FAITH TO THE SELF IN THE SELECT WORKS OF GABRIEL GARCIA MARQUEZ

A PSYCHOLOGICAL STUDY

DR. SREEJITH RAMACHANDRAN

Made with ❤ on the Notion Press Platform
www.notionpress.com

"To all those who took a stand and fought - conquered or succumbed to - Covid 19, their own deepest and purest desires, and the greatest illness of them all - Love."

Contents

Preface

Have you ever wondered what drives the characters in Gabriel Garcia Marquez's captivating novels? Why do they cling to hope with such unwavering tenacity? How does their fierce individualism shape their destinies? This book, "Unflinching Faith to the Self," embarks on a captivating exploration of these very questions.

We delve into the heart of five of Marquez's most celebrated works: No One Writes to the Colonel, One Hundred Years of Solitude, Love in the Time of Cholera, The General in His Labyrinth, and Of Love and Other Demons. Through the lens of psychology, we dissect the themes of individualism, hope, and illness that permeate these narratives.

Leon Festinger's Cognitive Dissonance Theory and Charles Richard Snyder's Hope Theory become our guiding lights as we navigate the intricate workings of the human mind within Marquez's fantastical realism. We witness the characters grapple with unwavering self-belief, the power of hope as a motivational force, and the challenges posed by both physical and mental illness.

This book is a treasure trove for those who seek:

- A deeper understanding of the psychological underpinnings of Marquez's characters.
- Insights into the complex interplay between individual desires and societal pressures.
- The exploration of hope and perseverance as catalysts for human achievement.
- An exploration of the impact of illness and the human capacity for resilience.

Within these pages, you'll discover:

- A comprehensive introduction to Latin American literature, with a particular focus on magical realism and its role in Marquez's works.

- A detailed analysis of the chosen novels, revealing the psychological motivations behind characters' actions and choices.
- An exploration of the theoretical frameworks used to understand the characters' mental states.
- A concluding chapter that summarizes key findings, offers fresh perspectives on Marquez's literary techniques, and proposes avenues for further research.

Let us embark on a psychological journey through the mesmerizing labyrinth of Gabriel Garcia Marquez's fictional worlds and unlock the secrets that lie beneath the surface, and gain a profound understanding of the human condition as depicted by this literary maestro.

Acknowledgements

First and foremost, I wish to place on record my heartfelt and sincere thanks to my supervisor **Dr. K. Rajkumar,** Assistant Professor, Department of English, Nehru Arts and Science College (Autonomous) for providing me an opportunity to pursue my Ph.D. thesis. I appreciate his effort and ideas to make my work productive. His invaluable suggestions and guidance encouraged me to learn more with each passing day. His vision and insights helped me at various phases of my study. I am also indebted to him for his generosity, selfless support and especially for the excellent example and patience during the course of the research.

It is with deep sense of gratitude that I thank **Dr. P. Krishna Kumar**, CEO and Secretary, Nehru Group of Institutions, **Dr. B. Anirudhan,** Principal, Nehru Arts and Science College (Autonomous), for providing me with a platform to undertake my research.

I extend my thanks to **Dr. R. Malathi,** Head, Department of English and Dean, School of Liberal Arts, Nehru Arts and Science College (Autonomous) for her never ending support and encouragement which inspired me to accomplish this task successfully.

A special thanks to **Dr. S.P. Sasirekha,** Associate Professor, Kongunadu Arts and Science College (Autonomous), Coimbatore, for conducting the Doctoral Committee meetings and providing insight and advice.

A word of thanks is due to **Dr. V. Shanmugam**, Research Director and **Dr. Mythili Gnanapriya**, Controller of Examinations, Nehru Arts and Science College (Autonomous), Coimbatore for their support during this study.

I am greatly obliged to **Dr.V.Kavitha**, Assistant Professor, Madanapally Institute of Technology and Science, Andhra Pradesh,

Dr. M. Devendran, Assistant Professor, and all the staff members of the Department of English, Nehru Arts and Science College (Autonomous) for their support and encouragement.

I thank **Mr. G. Ranjith**, Ph.D. Research Scholar and **Ms. Agalya. C. R**, M.Phil. Research Scholar, Department of English, for their support during the research.

I extend my gratitude to my wife **Dr.Gamaya.K.P**, Assistant Professor of English, for being my constant companion and always pushing me towards success. She has stood by me through all my travails, my fits of pique and impatience. The support she has rendered has brought out the best in me in all spheres of life. The discussions we have had presented me great many ideas and prevented several wrong turns. I thank her for her love, for all the late nights and early mornings, for keeping me sane over the past months, for being my muse and above all my best friend. I owe her everything.

I thank **the Librarians** of Nehru Arts and Science College (Autonomous), Bharathiar University, Coimbatore, Bharathidasan University - Thiruchirappalli, University of Calicut, SCILET Library – Madurai and British Council Library – Chennai for permitting me to make use of their library sources in an effective manner.

I could not have completed this academic exercise without the love and support of my family, I record my heartfelt gratitude to my dear parents **Mr. Ramachandran. P. T** and **Mrs. Sukannia. P. K,** for their blessing, unstinted support and large heartedness extended to me throughout during the course of study. A special word of appreciation is to my sister, **Mrs. Rajasree Subin**, my brother-in-law, **Mr. Subin. K. S** and my nephew **Master Sriram Seyon,** for the moral support to pursue this research. I also thank my father-in-law **Mr. K.P. Jayapalan**, mother-in-law **Mrs. Geetha Jayapalan** and brother- in-law **Mr. Kamal K.P.** for their kindness and understanding.

Finally, I thank God almighty for his choicest blessings in all my endeavours.

I express my sincere appreciation to those who have contributed to this book and supported me in one way or the other during this amazing journey, for without any of them, this work would not have been possible.

(Dr. Sreejith Ramachandran)

CHAPTER ONE

INTRODUCTION

"Literature is the one place in any society where, within the secrecy of our own heads, we can hear voices talking about everything in every possible way." – Salman Rushdie

In general, the term literature refers to written or spoken content. The term derives from the Latin words "littera" or "litteratura", which mean "writing formed with letters". It is most frequently used in creative works such as poetry, prose, plays, novels, and short stories. Journalism and song are occasionally considered literature as well. To put it in simple terms, literature symbolises a community's or language's customs and culture.

Numerous attempts have been made to define literature uniformly, but none have succeeded, as the definition appears to be ever-changing and transient. For a majority of the general public, literature is a more elevated form of art. For them, the meagre accumulation of words on paper is not synonymous with literary creation. A canon is a collection of works by a particular author. Certain literary works become canonical if they culturally represent a particular literary genre, such as prose, verse, or play.

Latin American Literature

Latin American literature encompasses oral and written works that originate in Latin America, written in a variety of dialects, including Portuguese, Spanish, indigenous languages of the two continents, and Spanish literature produced in the United States of America. It rose to prominence in the latter half of the twentieth century, owing largely to the global success of the literary technique known as Magical Realism. Latin American literature is frequently deeply rooted in this style, which was popularised by the Latin American Boom, a twentieth-century arts movement led by Gabriel Garcia Marquez. The rich and complex literary tradition of Latin America evolved over hundreds of years, and its merits are readily apparent to all who peruse it.

Latin American literature emerges as a result of the bizarre logical inconsistencies between patriotism and the domains that describe the locale's experience. Latin America's journey to independence, like that of all other states that were formerly colonies, involved a search for a distinct social and national character. In any case, this Latin American character is indefinable. It is distinguished by the conflict between the provincial power of Spanish predominance, the soul of disclosure and the quest to establish a new public with values and a new understanding of the scene and its uniqueness, and the proximity of non-European societies to the locale. While the literatures of the Latin American nations share some similarities, they are distinct in their own ways. The historical context of contemporary Latin American literature tends to homogenize and lump all nations into a solitary and rational unit; at the same time, it preserves each nation's unmistakable patriotism; the accounts of these nations converge on specific focuses, but remain quite distinct from one another. Despite the fact that Latin American authors came from diverse nationalistic backgrounds, they shared a common goal: to bring the soul of the soil bloodied over the centuries to light through literature.

Latin American literature is steeped in history. The colonial era, independence era, national solidification era, and contemporary era are the major epochs in Latin American literature's development. Throughout the colonial period, literature was influenced by its Spanish and Portuguese ancestors and primarily consisted of instructional compositions and historical annals. The mid-nineteenth century liberty movement ushered in an era of dynamic subjects presented in mostly beautiful structure. Following this period of consolidation, Romanticism, and Modernism were established, with expositions as the preferred mode of expression. Finally, in the mid-twentieth century, Latin American literature began to experiment with novel and dramatic forms.

Similarly, Spain and its foreign settlements assert that the earliest works of Latin American literature were composed in Spanish. War and Christianity's spread, as well as the organisation of the newly discovered continent, harmed the development of verse and fiction. In the majority of cases, sixteenth-century Spanish-American literature exceeds expectations in terms of instructional exposition works and historical accounts. The soul of the Spanish Renaissance, with its same stern intensity, is evident in the early pioneer period's compositions. Church men prevailed in every social endeavour. Mexico City and Lima were the epicentres of all intellectual movements in seventeenth-century New Spain and Peru. Urban social life, once a vital part of Spain's recreation, devolved into a daily routine of intelligence, service, and deception.

The popularity of Pedro Calderon de la Barcay Henao's and Luis de Gongora y Argote's works demonstrates the acceptance of contemporary literary styles. Juana Ines de la Cruz, a Mexican nun who wrote both religious and secular plays, was the most eminent seventeenth century writer. Additionally, she composed sonnets about women and personal writing about her various scholarly interests. A mixture of parody and practicality, which ebbed and flowed in Spanish literature at the time, manifested itself similarly abroad, both in verse and fiction.

In 1700, the Habsburg line in Spain was supplanted by the Bourbon line. This occasion with or without authentic authorization exposed the settlements to French influences, resulting in widespread recognition of French elegance and the Enlightenment's libertarian teachings. Jose Joaquin Fernandez de Lizardi, dubbed "the Mexican Thinker", was a pamphleteer and author who travelled with a portable printing press, churning out material on the independence movement's side. His debut novel, The Itching Parrot, sparked a local wave of sentimental fiction.

Despite the fact that the congregation in Spain used the picaresque classification to teach morality, Lizardi's picaresque novel was vehemently anti-clerical.

Adaptations of French plays were the major contribution of Peralta Barnuevo, a Peruvian author. Various other writers, including Francisco Eugenio from Ecuador and Antonio Narino of Colombia, contributed to the spread of progressive ideas in late-eighteenth century France. Furthermore, during this time period, new scholarly foci emerged. Ecuador's Quito, Colombia's Bogota, Venezuela's Caracas, and Argentina's Buenos Aires began competing in education, manufacturing, and scholarly social affairs with the old vice-regal capitals. Contacts with non-Spanish speakers increased, testing the region's scholarly imposing business model.

During the struggle for liberty, an explosion of patriotic literature occurred, the majority of which was written in verse. Jose Joaquin Fernandez wrote the magnum opus of Spanish-American literature, Periquillo Sarmiento. In it, the experiences of a cunning hero offset the cost of all-encompassing perspectives on pioneer life that obscure societal reactions. Due to the acceptance of scholars as tribunes of the Roman republic during this period, literature and politics were inextricably linked. In his sonnet 'Victoria de Junin', Ecuadorian artist and political pioneer Jose Joaquin Olmedo extols the virtues of South American progressive pioneer, warrior, and statesman Simon Bolivar. Venezuelan author Andres Bello lauded tropical horticulture in his well-known Silvas Americanas, a collection of rural verse akin to those of Virgil. Cuban artist Jose Maria de Heredia y Campuzano foreshadowed the demise of sentimentalism in sonnets such as 'Al Niagara', written while he was an outcast in the United States. Simultaneously, a mysterious well-known political verse gained popularity among the La Plata district's gauchos.

During the consolidation period, the new Latin American republics viewed France more favourably than Spain, albeit with a more nativistic bent. Traditional structures of the eighteenth century provided a counterpoint to sentimentalism, which dominated much of the nineteenth century. Esteban Echeverria initiated Argentina into the world of French- European sentimentalism. French influence permeated Mexico, while costumbrista works preserved the Hispanic practical tradition. Numerous Spanish-American journalists took part in political and financial alliances and battles during this time period. The alleged Argentine sentimentalist rebel-uprising age of Dictator Juan Manuel de Rosas's opponents was imminent. Jose Marmol, author of the shroud-and-knife sentiment *Amalia*, was present at this gathering, which influenced Chile and Uruguay as well. Jose Marmol's work was influenced by the works of Sir Walter Scott and Alexandre Dumas. Domingo Faustino Sarmiento, a teacher (and later President of Argentina), whose authentic social examination Facundo demonstrated that Latin America's fundamental problem was a schism between its primitive state and European influences.

Novel was making significant strides at that moment. Alberto Blest Gana, a Chilean, transitioned from sentimentalism to authenticity in his *Martin Rivas* by delineating Chilean culture using Balzacian systems. The story exemplifies his desire to become Chile's Balzac, despite the fact that it is fundamentally a romantic work rather than a practical one. To be honest, it has been dubbed the best example of Romantic authenticity in Latin America, and it exemplifies the typical extremes found in his period's literature: city versus nation, reality versus appearances, and great versus malicious characters. *Cumanda*, by Juan Leon Mera, immortalised the setting of Indian wilderness in Ecuador. Mera establishes the framework for an advanced novel of dissent against the Indians' brutal treatment, about whom he had strong narrative information, in *Cumanda*.

A novel of a similar style, tinged with European sentimentality and replete with pivotal fortuitous events and exaggerated astonishments, including the standard incomprehensible marriage of kin, appeared in Peru under the title *Birds Without a Nest: A Story of Indian Life and Priestly Opposition in Peru.* Clorinda Matto de Turner, the author, also included an introduction within the convention of the moralistic exposition, stating that her motivation was to demonstrate the Peruvian Indian's unjust treatment. It is a textbook example of a nineteenth-century romantic story in that it is unmistakably concerned with subject rather than procedure.

Ignacio Altamirano was a remarkable sentimental pragmatist in Mexico. He sought to elevate the status of the Latin American epic by encouraging his individual writers to read widely in order to foster a more inclusive artistic vision. While he was an Indian himself dedicated to making the novel more reasonable, he tended to create impractically stereotyped characters, whether Indian or otherwise, and neglected to argue the Indian's case vehemently. *Clementia and Christmas in the Mountains* are both excellent books, but *El Zarco: the Bandit* demonstrates his ability to write an action-packed adventure story. *El Zarco* features two couples, one positive and one negative, one highlighting what Mexico has to offer and the other highlighting what it is attempting to eradicate. Naturalistic writers, such as Argentine Eugenio Cambaceres, author of *Sin Rumbo*, emulated the impact of French author Emile Zola's trial books.

In the 1880s, innovation emerged as a development of conceptual revival. It benefited significantly from the political and economic integration of Latin American republics, as well as the resulting harmony and prosperity among larger nations. It emphasised the purely creative aspects of literature over the purely utilitarian ones. It was defined by refined sensibilities, even hyper-aestheticism, and its objective was to transcend rather than comprehend Latin American reality. The pioneers shared a cosmopolitan culture influenced by late European patterns, particularly French Parnassian and symbolist verse; their works incorporated past and present, external and indigenous structures and subjects.

The spread of innovation from Latin America to Spain, which ended around 1910, left its mark on exposition fiction, emphasising the author's imaginative ability and expanding the author's use of symbolism in composition style, culminating in certain books that must be read almost as verse due to the force of their language. Simultaneously, a sizable proportion of authors eschewed innovation in favour of practical or naturalistic works on territorial social issues.

Ricardo Guiraldes from Argentina wrote territorial fiction in *DonSegundoSombra*, the conclusion to his gaucho novel; Jose Eustasio Rivera from Colombia wrote wilderness fiction in *La Vordgine*; and Romulo Gallegos from Venezuela wrote field fiction in *Dona Barbara*. Miguel Angel Asturias, Guatemala's ambassador who won the Lenin Peace

Prize in 1966 and the Nobel Prize in Literature in 1967, exceeded expectations in *El Senor Presidente* as a political comedian. Jorge Luis Borges, Argentina's first avant- garde artist, rose to prominence as the country's best known author as a specialist in strange supernatural tales. Additionally, his works lend themselves to a variety of interpretations. He sparked interest in contemporary criminologist narrative and dream literature, along with Adolfo Bioy Casares.

Rayuela, by Julio Cortazar, received widespread acclaim. Cortazar's works have received widespread acclaim for their brilliance and singularity. Due to the influence of British scholars Virginia Woolf and Aldous Huxley, Irish essayist James Joyce, and, most notably, American journalists John Dos Passos and William Faulkner, the new Mexican story departed from unimportant rough authenticity. Jose Revueltas composed *Human Mourning* within a provincial framework, and Agustin Yanez composed *The Edge of the Storm*, which included new mental and mysterious measurements. *Where the Air is Clear* by Carlos Fuentes oscillates between the absolutely phenomenal and the nativistic.

Since 1900, three explicit facets of the Latin American story in Spanish have been portrayed: the pragmatist innovator duality, super-regionalism, and the pursuit of universalisation. The pragmatist pioneer pattern persisted until 1910, the year of Mexico's average law-based insurgency. This occasion struck a chord with Latin American authors. Their capacity to perceive and delineate the brutal reality that the pioneers attempted to conceal necessitated the use of pragmatist composition. Regardless, artistic authenticity in the Latin American context required the depiction of the region's peculiar issues and clashes, which is how the passing term 'regionalism' was coined.

The authors grasped for an understanding of the American situation, searching for explanations for their financial plight and the wretchedness of their kin. This resulted in their works exaggerating the conflict between human advancement and brutality. Nature versus development became a point of convergence in the writing of fiction. Social issues continued to reverberate, but nature was portrayed as an all powerful force in their works.

The period from World War I to 1950 left an indelible mark on the people of Latin America. Latin American essayists were legitimately informed about the Spanish Civil War under one-party rule, and the Spanish Republic's demise in 1936 was a deeply felt personal tragedy for them. On a financial level, the improvement of industry, however marginal, resulted in the growth of urban centres and the rise of indigenous elites. Whatever the case, any hopes for national renaissance were dashed as the Americans' intervention and exploitation of Latin America's natural resources proceeded efficiently. The situation was complicated by political brutality and the erosion of popular rights. Contrary to the reality of Hispanic America's underdevelopment, a fictitious picture of Hispanic America's advancement was anticipated. Such degraded conditions that are prevalent in the public eye will undoubtedly find their way into masterpieces and literature.

The transition from a regionalist or confined perspective on issues and clashes to a more expansive perspective on reality, that is, within the system of power relations at the global level, became unavoidable. Scholars were neither intrigued nor convinced by the apparent rapture of progress in the landmass. They were now capable of recognising the danger posed by the states of confusion and insecurity that had engulfed their district. The threat of neo-colonialism proved to be abundantly genuine and obvious to them, particularly in light of the US's financial and social infiltration of the lives of Latin American people groups. The issue of Man versus Nature, which had dominated the landmass's literature up to this point, typically subsided out of view, paving the way for the depiction of man trapped in the soil of moral and financial conflict.

By and large, Latin American writers in Spanish have achieved global recognition through the development of new complex systems, styles, points of view, and topics that transcend traditional regionalism. The elaborate label, magical realism, is applicable to a sizable proportion of more grounded storytellers, those who appear to convey a sense of the secret hidden behind the real world. During the 1960's, an unlikely group of scholars rose to prominence. During this period, the introduction of the 'New Latin American Novel' is frequently referred to as the 'boom' of Latin American literature. Alejo Carpentier, a Cuban author, added another fanciful dimension to the wilderness novel with his novel *The Lost Steps*. He discusses tyranny in his book Reasons of State. He creates an incredible impact in the novel by describing the despot through the use of internal monologue.

Mario Vargas Llosa of Peru discovered numerous perspectives in the seemingly closed universe of a military school in *The Time of the Hero*. The military, prostitution or a combination of the two were the subjects of the majority of his works. Joao Guimaraes Rosa's *The Devil to Pay in the Backlands* is written in a Joycean style, replete with neologisms and local dialect. Jose Donoso, a Chilean author frequently compared to Llosa, is best known for his evocative conclusion *The Obscene Bird of Night*. Donoso's books reflect a shift in the writer's specialty in his country while also adhering to the country's tradition of analysing a segment of the general public through the use of painstakingly controlled language.

Julio Cortazar's works are a significant example of the generalisation of the Latin American epic. His epic, Hopscotch, departs from the sterile milieu of his generation's Argentine literature and introduces an unmistakably progressive bonafide existentialist saint in Horacio Oliveira. Oliveira is a moving individual who creates another persona, however flawed, as he does so. One of Cortazar's most significant commitments to the new novel is his invitation for the reader to participate in the inventive demonstration alongside him. The Latin American epic in Spanish, as crafted by these journalists, matured, but also appeared to dazzle an expanding global open, as a most incredible development of general intrigue.

For a long period of time in Colombia's literature, Jorge Isaac's *Maria* and Jose Eustacia Rivera's *La Vordgine* were the two works that dominated the country's middle phase. *Maria*, a verse story about fated love on an old ranch, is a masterpiece of Hispanic art among sentimental books. Jorge Isaac and 'other sentimental figures were frequently concerned with nature, and the courageous woman of Isaac's epic bears all the hallmarks of being a near-example of Colombia's Cauca Valley. The story is typical of its day, including an encounter with two perfect partners who are isolated and then reunited at the conclusion, only to discover that destiny has rendered their marriage unthinkable. Currently, the couple is sibling and sister through appropriation, and her death precludes their marriage.

The work entitled *One Hundred Years of Solitude* by Garcia Marquez, and other works fundamentally altered the way Latin American commentators and readers assessed their country's legacy. His books materialise out of thin air, leaping beyond the generally defined boundaries of Latin American literature to become global marvels. With his new story systems, he de-regionalizes, de-nationalizes, and internationalises Latin American literature. His ability to create works of significance that accomplish both fundamental and well-known goals has shattered national artistic boundaries and catapulted Latin American literature to the forefront of scholarly development.

Following that, Colombian writer Garcia Marquez elevated the Latin American novel to new heights by elevating it above the mundane world through enchanted and eternal solidarity. Colombia's history is littered with savage and bloody episodes, and Garcia Marquez witnessed a number of them, which he depicts in his books.

A Snippet of the Author's Biography

It was in a house full of endless aunts and phantom gossips that on March 26, 1928, Gabriel Garcia Marquez was born in Aracataca, Colombia. His adolescence was happy, wherein he was raised by his maternal grandparents in a narrative domain, where elders were constantly recalling and telling stories about the family's and the town's historical background. Colonel N. Marquez, his grandfather, was on the liberal side and against the victorious sect who were Conservatives during the Thousand Days' War. Being the final instalment of the perpetual civil wars that leased Colombia, he frequently reflected on those turbulent times. As uncritical and superstitious women, his grandmother and aunts believed in the supernatural and related a wide variety of otherworldly occurrences as if they were commonplace. The author has stated numerous times that his grandmother inspired his story.

Garcia Marquez discovered in law school that he lacked enthusiasm for his legal studies. By skipping classes, he developed contempt for both his academics and for himself. He took the streetcars and strolled through Bogota's streets. He read *the Bible* rather than the law. In any case, a book he read turned his life upside down. *The Metamorphosis* by Franz Kafka profoundly influenced Garcia Marquez and made him realise that literature does not have to be linear or predictable. It was emancipating, because he recognised his ability to write immediately. He would have started writing years ago had he been aware of the opportunity earlier. He states that his grandmother's voice truly resembled that of Franz Kafka. His grandmother used to tell him completely ordinary stories about the strangest of events. He read the entire body of literature he had avoided due to Kafka's influence.

He began insatiably perusing, consuming whatever came his way. He started writing fiction and his first work named *The Third*

Resignation, was published in 1946 by the liberal Bogota newspaper El Espectador. Over the next few years, he initiated his creative era, contributing ten additional accounts to the newspaper.

The two authors who had the greatest influence on him were William Faulkner and Sophocles. He was awestruck by Faulkner's ability to transform his youth into a legendary past through the establishment of a town and setting for his work. He discovered the seeds of Macondo in Faulkner's fabled *Yoknapatawpha* and Sophocles' *Oedipus Rex*, where plot revolves around the general public and intensity is mistreated. Garcia Marquez was not content with his earlier works, believing them to be far deferred from his own experiences. He considered them to be merely deft embellishments that bore no resemblance to reality. Garcia Marquez devoted an inordinate amount of time to deciphering what Faulkner meant when he stated that an essayist should expound on the personal.

Even his earlier works, *No One Writes to the Colonel, Leaf Storm,* and *In Evil Hour*, possessed an apathetic and singular quality. *No One Writes to the Colonel* and *Leaf Storm* turned too far from the idea that he had been working on for years. According to him, his most significant work would happen in the legendary town of Macondo and he needed to find the right quality for telling his story; he needed to find his true voice. Finally, in 1965, he was struck by an unexpected motivation, which enabled him to establish the tone of his novel.

In a long while, Macondo's voice was initially revealed by a bolt of lightning. He began writing and continued for eighteen months. *One Hundred Years of Solitude*, a work that was published in 1967, was quickly sold out. Success was assured from that time, being the novel sold out another edition every week for three years, eventually selling over a million copies. It has been translated into more than 37 dialects and won four international awards.

Garcia Marquez embodies magical realism. He is an expert at transforming the extraordinary into genuine presence. He lends authenticity to enchantment by fusing the phenomenal and the real. He incorporates surprising episodes into everyday life with mystical authenticity. He achieves enchantment authenticity by exaggerating the events. Regardless, the distortion is frequently numerically explicit, and each event is transformed into a sense of the real world. Magical realism is frequently associated with fictions that depict those on the periphery of political power and powerful society. It is honed in a substantial number of postcolonial nations that are contending with the legacy of their former provincial rulers and believe themselves to be on the verge of magnificent force. With his enchanting authenticity, he seeks to unearth the genuine reality that has been obscured by historians, political forces, and prevalent ideal models imposed by high culture.

The truth he reveals compels colonised countries to re-evaluate genuine reality, rejecting the prevailing ideal models imposed by political and other forces. These ideal models are predefined concepts that exist in incontrovertible and unchallengeable circumstances. He depicts a befuddled and dubious world in which clashes emerge as a result of an extraordinary desire to preserve ethnic identity and social political structure, despite abuse from those who pull the strings. To put it plainly, he needs to demonstrate in his books that 'other' societies have a unique value based on their indigenous legends and superstitions. Garcia Marquez is the author of numerous magnificent novels and novellas. The books chosen for this study are *Of Love and Other Demons, No One Writes to the Colonel, The General in His Labyrinth, Love in the Time of Cholera,* and *One Hundred Years of Solitude.*

Contemporaries of the Author

The moustachioed Colombian wound up venturing into the progressive issues of an unexpected, frail, and potentially hostile locale, much like Carlos Fuentes, Isabel Allende, Mario Vargas Llosa, Victor Jara, and Pablo Neruda did.

Carlos Fuentes Macias was a Mexican essayist and author who was born on November 11, 1928, in Mexico City. His works include *The Death of Artemio Cruz* (1962), *Aura* (1962), *Terra Nostra* (1975), *The Old Gringo* (1985), and *Christopher Unborn* (1985). The

New York Times rated Fuentes as well acknowledged and revered writers who is in the Spanish-speaking countries, a pivotal figure in the 1960s and 1970s surge of Latin American literature, alongside, The Guardian calls him as most acclaimed novelist of Mexico. He was frequently mentioned as a possible Literature Nobel Laureate, but never won.

On 2nd August 1942, Isabel Angelica Allende Llona was born in Peru. Allende is considered best known for his commercial successes *The House of the Spirits* (1982) as well as *The City of the Beasts* (1984). Allende received the 2010 Chilean National Literature Prize and was also included in the year 2004 into the American Academy of Arts and Letters. She is named as a Spanish author whose work is extensively read worldwide. The Presidential Medal of Freedom was conferred to her in the year 2014 by the then President Barack Obama. Her novels are largely based on historical events and personal experience, with a particular emphasis on the lives of women through myth along with realism. She has spoken at colleges and universities across the country and taught literature.

Mario Vargas Llosa was the first Marquis of Vargas Llosa, born in Lima, Peru on March 28, 1936. He has worked as a writer, journalist, essayist, and college professor in addition to being a former politician. Vargas Llosa, a renowned novelist from Latin American and essayist who is considered as well acknowledged influential writers of his era. According to some of the literary critics, he had a greater cultural impact and fan base than any other Latin American famous author. In the year 2010, the prestigious Nobel Prize in Literature was awarded for his mapping of special power models and sharp depictions of resistance by individuals, insurgency, and failure.

Victor Lidio Jara Martnez was a Chilean teacher, poet, theatre director, songwriter, singer, and communist political activist who was tormented and murdered during the autocracy of Augusto Pinochet. He shaped the Chilean theatre through his direction of a diverse range of works, including original works, international classics, and experimental works by authors such as Ann Jellicoe.

Additionally, he was a pivotal figure in Chile's neo-folkloric musicians' movement, Nueva Cancion Chilena (New Chilean Song). This resulted in a burst of new sounds in popular music during President Salvador Allende's presidency.

Pablo Neruda was a politician, poet and a diplomat from Chile, who won the Nobel Prize in Literature in the year 1971. On 12 July 1904, Ricardo Eliecer Neftali Reyes Basoalto was born and died on 23 September 1973. His works include surrealist poetry, historical epics, politically charged manifestos which are an autobiography which is written in prose, and wrote some love poems which are so passionate, *Twenty Love Poems* and another work *A Song of Despair* published in 1924. Chile's national poet, Pablo Neruda, is well-known, and his writings have influenced people throughout the world. In his book The Western Canon, Harold Bloom talked about Neruda as the finest poet that the twentieth century has ever witnessed. In addition, Gabriel Garcia Marquez considered him as the greatest poet in any language so far written in any language in the twentieth century.

Plot Synopses of the Selected Novels

No One Writes to the Colonel is a work about a veteran in his late-seventies, who served as a colonel during Colombia's Thousand Days' War in the late twentieth century. The colonel along with his elderly wife lived in a decaying town overrun by rude political savagery, corrupt officials, and elite individuals. Decades ago, despite his pivotal role in the Thousand Days' War, transporting the trunks stuffed with cashes for the civil war roped on the back of a mule. The Colonel has never received his benefits checks.

Despite his tragic situations, the colonel remains relentless in waiting for his checks, walking down to the harbour's mail station during Fridays. The postmaster disappoints him by saying that no one is interested in writing to the colonel. The colonel's wife also recognises that the annuity is a distant hope that after a period of disillusionment and near-starvation, informs her husband that they cannot survive by eating 'hope'.

The short story welcomes the readers with the death of a young man, which was considered as a natural death that happened first in the town. The Colonel's son, Augustin, was assassinated by fighters because of the distribution of clandestine literature. The Colonel could get a chicken from Augustin to use in cockfighting. The chicken has a chance to earn money if it fights well, but the elderly couple cannot bear the cost of sustaining both the chicken and themselves. But the colonel's wife regards the chicken as an illusion that is too expensive. The colonel is seen as placing greater trust in its outcome than he does in his annuity.

The colonel and his wife never compromised their pride and nobility even when they were living in dire starvation. He was not ready to sell any of his belongings even in this difficult situation. Sabas, his companion who had become rich travelling through political devotions by his wife's instruction, was offered chicken. On the contrary, the colonel got back his chicken disregarding his office. Eventually, in the short story, at the inquiry of his wife's concern about having food, the colonel responds that they would eat 'shit'.

The Buendia family's founding of Macondo, a remote town has been detailed in *One Hundred Years of Solitude*. For years, the town was cut off from the rest of the world by gypsies who came to sell ice and telescopes. The family patriarch, Jose Arcadio Buendia, is a reckless and curious individual. As a result of his obsessive research into mysterious matters, he has remained an intensely solitary leader who has alienated himself from other men. Throughout the novel, these characteristics are passed down to his lineage. His elder son, Jose Arcadio, is seen as impressively inheriting his father's physical strength and impulsive nature. Aureliano, his younger son, inherited his mystique and intensity of concentration.

As contact with other towns in the region is established, the village's innocent, isolated state gradually erodes. In Macondo, civil war erupts, bringing violence and death, and Aureliano rises to become the leader of the Liberal rebels, earning the title of Colonel

Aureliano Buendia. As a result of Colonel Buendia's celebrity, Macondo irreversibly changes to a town permanently connected to the outside world from an idyllic, magical, and sheltered setting. Throughout and after the war, Macondo's governments changed numerous times. Before being executed by firing squad, Arcadio, the most atrocious of the Buendias, for a time showed his dictatorship. Eventually, an appointment of a mayor relatively made his reign peaceful until he was also assassinated during a civil war. Following his death, a peace treaty was signed to end the civil war.

Garcia Marquez describes the majority of events in the Buendias' lives as watershed moments: births, deaths, marriages, and love affairs, as the novel spans more than a century. Certain men from Buendia clan are hedonistic and sexually rapacious, frequently frequenting brothels and seducing women. Others are more reserved and solitary, preferring to spend their time alone in their rooms creating miniature golden fish or poring over old manuscripts. Women range in personality from the outgoing Meme, who once brought seventy two boarding school friends home, to the formal and suitable Fernanda del Carpio, who consummates her marriage in a special nightgown with a hole in the crotch.

Ursula Iguaran, the family's tenacious matriarch, is convinced of the family's destiny for greatness and works tirelessly to keep the family together despite their differences. However, modernity's centrifugal forces destroy the whole village of Macondo, and the family of Buendia. In Macondo, a banana plantation establishes itself, exploiting the land and its workers, and the plantation's owners construct a fenced-in section of town. The banana pickers eventually stage a strike in protest of their inhumane treatment. Tens of thousands are slaughtered by the army who support the plantation owners. Soon after the bodies are dumped into the sea, continuous rain begins for five years culminating in a flood that destroys Macondo. As the city fades away as a result of years of violence and false progress, the Buendia family, overcome by nostalgia for bygone eras, initiates its own final erasure. The novel concludes almost exactly as it began: the village again turns lonely and isolated. A few remaining Buendia family members withdraw incestuously and stay isolated from the outer world and are destined to live in isolation. The novel's final scene depicts the lone Buendia survivor deciphering a series of prophecies and discovering that every incident that happened had been predicted as the characters of the village and the people living there had simply been a part of a predetermined sequence marked by elegance and tragic depth.

In the famous work, *LoveintheTimeofCholera*, Florentino Ariza and Fermina Daza play the role of protagonists. Florentino and Fermina begin to reflect on their youth. With the assistance of Fermina's aunt Escolastica, Fermina and Florentino develop a strange relationship. They exchange a handful of heartfelt letters. When Lorenzo Daza, Fermina's father, learns more about the two, he advises his daughter to immediately stop seeing Florentino. When his diseased wife becomes unable to care for herself, he and his daughter relocate to another city to live with her family. Fermina and Florentino maintain contact through broadcast despite their separation. Fermina's arrival convinces her that her relationship with Florentino was a fantasy; she cancels their engagement and returns all of Florentino's letters.

Dr. Juvenal Urbino, a rising national legend, meets and courts Fermina. Fermina, despite her dislike for Urbino, succumbs to her father's influence and the security and wealth that Urbino provides, and the two marry. Urbino is a physician who is committed to science, progress, and the concept of "demand and progress". He is an advocate for cholera eradication and social advancement. He is a rational man who has planned his life meticulously and places a premium on his public stature. He is the harbinger of change and progress. Florentino pledged to be loyal to Fermina following her commitment and marriage.

Regardless, his apathy indicates that he is making progress. He ensures that Fermina will never find out his infidelity, regardless of how many ladies he is with. Fermina and Urbino then grow old together, sharing happy and unhappy years and confronting all of the marriage's difficulties. Urbino falls from his stepping ladder and dies in his old age while attempting to free his pet parrot from his mango tree. Florentino professes his love for Fermina once more following the burial service, assuring her that he has remained faithful to her over the years. She is hesitant to begin due to her recent loss, and she also discovers and dismisses his inappropriate advances. In the end, Fermina grants him another chance. They make an attempt at a new life together after living two separate lives for over five decades.

After several years of marriage, Urbino finally admits to Fermina that he was not an entirely devoted spouse. While the novel implies that Urbino's feelings for Fermina were never as strong as Florentino's, it also casts doubt on Florentino's commitment by relegating his numerous trysts to a few possibly genuine love affairs. Fermina gains an appreciation for Florentino's knowledge and development prior to the book's conclusion, and their love blossoms during their mature years.

The General in His Labyrinth is told through the eyes of an outsider, with vignettes depicting significant events in the life of Simon Bolivar, "the General". It all started on May 8, 1830, in Santa Fe de Bogota. The General is en route to Cartagena de Indias, from which he will travel to Europe. Residents of the grounds he liberated have turned on him, spray painting anti-Bolvar graffiti and throwing waste at him following his resignation as President of Gran Colombia. The General is eager to proceed, but must remind Vice President- elect General Domingo Caycedo that he has not yet received a valid passport authorising him to leave the country. The General leaves Bogota with only a few of his personal staff members remaining, including his compatriot and confidant, Jose Palacios. Near the novel's conclusion, the General is addressed by his given name: Bolivar y Palacios, General Simon Jose Antonio de la Santisima Trinidad

The General's first night in Facatativa is spent with Jose Palacios, five confidants, his assistants, and his canines. As is the case throughout the excursion, the General's decline in renown is obvious; even the General is surprised by his fortunes' decline. His unidentified disease has rendered him physically unrecognisable, and his confidant is frequently confused with the Liberator.

The General and his entourage arrive in Honda following numerous postponements, where Governor Posada Gutierrez has organised three days of festivities. On his final night in Honda, the General returns late to camp and is greeted by one of his old companions, Miranda Lyndsay. The General recalls how she discovered and foiled an assassination plot against him fifteen years ago. The following morning, the General embarks on his journey down the Magdalena. While arranging the incline to the dock, he demonstrates his physical frailty and pride. He is in desperate need of a sedan chair but will not use one. The celebration organised in his honour continues into the night in Puerto Real, where the General claims to have seen a woman singing in the darkness. His confidants and the gatekeeper search the area but find no evidence of a female presence.

The General and his men proceed to Mompox's port, where they are apprehended by unaware police. They demand his passport, which he cannot produce. He is eventually apprehended and transported to the port by the police. Individuals trust him regardless of the circumstances and prepare meals for him; however, due to his lack of solidarity and hunger, these celebrations are meaningless to him. The General and his company reached Turbaco after a few days.

Prior to their arrival in Turbaco, the group spends an anxious night in Barranca Nueva. Their unique arrangement required them to stay in Cartagena the following day, but the General is informed that there is no boat to Europe accessible from the port and that his visa has not arrived despite everything. While he is still in town, General Mariano Montilla and a few others pay him a visit. His health deteriorates to the point where one of his guests paints his face in the likeness of a dead man. General Daniel Florencio O'Leary arrives in Turbaco to brief the General on current political intrigues: While Joaquin Mosquera, the designated successor to Gran Colombia's President, has accepted the use of force, General Rafael Urdaneta continues to cast doubt on his legitimacy. According to the General, his fantasy began self-destructing as soon as it became a reality.

Following the acquisition of a passport, the General and his escort travel to Cartagena and the coast, where additional gatherings, in his honour, are held. Throughou this time period, he is surrounded by ladies, but is too frail to contemplate sexual relations. When the General learns of Field Marshal Sucre's capture and assassination, he is moved to tears. The General has been informed by one of his confidants that General Rafael Urdaneta has seized control of the Bogota legislature, and reports have surfaced of demonstrations and uproar on the eve of Bolivar's arrival to take control. The General's gathering continues to Soledad, where he remains for more than a month, his health rapidly deteriorating. The General consents to a consultation with a physician in Soledad. The General is never seen outside of South America. He is unable to continue his journey in Santa Marta due to his frail health and the presence of only his aides de camp and closest associates. He dies a destitute and destitute death, a sad relic of the man who liberated a sizable portion of the continent.

Of Love and Other Demons is the story of a twelve-year-old girl's life and death. The hair of the Marquis and his wife Bernarda's twelve-year-old daughter has never been cut and was guaranteed to the holy people upon her birth with the umbilical cord wrapped around her neck. She was brought up by slaves and is fluent in a variety of African dialects and traditions. At the novel's start, she is bitten by a rabid canine. Despite her lack of rabies symptoms, she is subjected to a variety of "mending" techniques that can be interpreted as torment. She is sent to the Santa Clara community in order to secure an expulsion that has resulted in the deaths of numerous residents. She is examined by a priest, Father Cayetano, who is compassionate toward her and initially agrees not to exorcise her.

Father Cayetano falls hopelessly in love with Sierva Maria and professes his love for her; he quickly begins secretly visiting Sierva in her cell, sneaking up from the sewer (that in future is fixed). Despite their omission from the text, they eat, rest, and discuss verse in unison. Father Cayetano is later admitted to a leprosy hospital, where he wishes to contract the disease but never does. Meanwhile, Sierva Maria is the final person to be exorcised, and she inevitably succumbs 'of adoration', while contemplating Father Cayetano's whereabouts and following her hair cropping. Her hair mysteriously regrows on her skull following her demise.

Aim and Objectives of the Study

The vast majority of people in this generation lack will power and determination. At the first sign of defeat, they abandon their desires and ambitions. They require constant motivation in order to stay on track. They should be educated about the various methods for developing inner strength and drive, as well as the various sources of motivation.

Garcia Marquez's major characters are frequently obstinate in their ambitions and desires. The majority of them remain steadfast in their convictions and never yield to the wishes or suggestions of others. Their motivation appears to be extremely enigmatic. The purpose of this study is to ascertain the motivations of the characters and the source of their hope. This way, today's generation may be able to develop strategies for defending their beliefs and pursuing their ambitions, ultimately leading to a life of contentment.

The major objectives of this book are the following:

- To find the motivating factors behind people's goal setting
- To analyse the influence of psychological factors in a person's goal setting
- To find the support structure of the person's determination and hope

- To understand the relation between happiness and success
- To study the effect of individualism in achieving success
- To come up with survival strategies for disheartening situations
- To analyse the need of achieving balance between inner and outer world
- To surmise a set of postulates for contentment in life

Research Problems

The majority of characters in these works are tenacious in their pursuit of life objectives. They cling to it in the hope that they will succeed. The causes of this optimism and hope are unknown. Even in the face of adversity, the characters remain steadfast in their pursuit of their objectives. This is the subject of this book. This book has the potential to benefit society in a variety of ways. Without a doubt, motivation is required for an individual to live a happy life. However, certain factors can contribute to a person becoming fixated on unachievable goals. This can result in dissatisfaction with life and a low sense of self-esteem. As a result, identifying motivational grey areas is critical. This study can assist in determining the effect of motivation and thus in resolving the preceding issue. This book propounds the idea that, objective oriented individualism devoid of obsession can lead one to a life of contentment, and hope coupled with tireless effort is the fuel to move forward in life.

Theories Adopted for the Study

Psychological theories are applied to the topics studied in this research. The study's major theories are Festinger's Cognitive Dissonance Theory and Snyder's Hope Theory.

Leon Festinger was the first to investigate cognitive dissonance. According to theory, we have an innate desire to maintain harmony in all our attitudes and behaviours and to avoid discord. This is referred to as the cognitive consistency principle. The theory was developed as a result of research into a cult that believed the earth would be destroyed by a flood and what happened to its members when the flood did not occur. This theory is used to examine the aspect of individualism displayed by the majority of the major characters in the chosen works.

Hope Theory of Charles Richard Snyder incorporates objectives, paths, and the ability to choose. He worked in the United States of America as a positive psychology specialist. His work in clinical, social, personality, and health psychology garnered international acclaim. He developed theories about human responses to personal feedback, the desire for uniqueness, and the hope motive during the 1980s and 1990s. Additional research was conducted on the basis of Snyder's findings to determine the relationship between increased hope and academic and athletic performance, as well as physical health and well-being. When individuals are aided in developing into so-called high-hopers, their outlook on life becomes more optimistic. This theory is applied to the study's selected works in order to examine the central theme of hope.

Chapter Summaries

This book is divided into six chapters. The introductory chapter, titled 'Introduction', provides context for the research. To aid in comprehension, the study's broad field of literature, genre, author biography, the novels under examination, the study's aims and objectives, research problems, and thesis statement are highlighted.

Chapter II, titled 'An Overview of the Theory', establishes the theoretical framework. The history and development of psychology, as well as the relationship between literature and psychology, are all explained in detail. This chapter discusses the theories that guided this study. Leon Festinger's Cognitive Dissonance Theory and Charles Richard Snyder's Hope Theory are the two theories.

Leon Festinger pioneered the study of Cognitive Dissonance Theory. When contradictory attitudes, beliefs, or behaviours exist, cognitive dissonance occurs. According to this theory, an internal drive binds our attitudes and behaviours together and keeps them from becoming discordant (or dissonance). Three primary factors contribute to dissonance: i) Compulsory Compliance; ii) Decision Making; and iii) Effort.

Hope Theory was developed by Charles Richard Snyder as a result of his research into the psychological effects of hope. Hope, he asserts, enhances an individual's attitude toward life (resulting in high achievements). Hope Theory encapsulates goals, paths, and the capacity to choose. It is composed of three elements: i) the individual must have clear objectives; ii) the individual must plan ahead to accomplish these objectives; and iii) the individual must be motivated to exert the effort necessary to accomplish these objectives.

Chapter III is titled 'Individualism: A Path to Happiness'. This chapter examines the concept of individualism, which defines a majority of Garcia Marquez's characters. The chapter applies Leon Festinger's Cognitive Dissonance Theory to the novels No One Writes to the Colonel, One Hundred Years of Solitude, Love in the Time of Cholera, The General in His Labyrinth, and Of Love and Other Demons. Individualism is a practice or a philosophy that emphasizes self-reliance and independence. As can be seen, the protagonists of each of these novels are highly individualistic. They remain steadfast in their commitment to their own beliefs and values, even at the risk of their lives. The result is not always favourable.

Chapter IV, 'Hope as a Motivational Factor', delves into the recurring theme of hope and despair in Garcia Marquez's works. This chapter makes use of the Hope Theory of Charles Richard Snyder. Hope is an emotion associated with anticipating and desiring a particular outcome. The majority of Marquez's characters are motivated by hope. While the majority of characters harbour and work toward positive goals, others merely hope.

Those who endure adversity succeed, while those who give up hope perish.

In Chapter V, titled 'Illness – Combating and Surviving', the term "illness" is used to refer to a physical (or mental) disorder or discomfort in a human, animal, or plant, more specifically one that produces specific symptoms and is not the result of physical injury. In the majority of Marquez's novels, disease is a sub-theme. The majority of the novels are set during modern medicine's infancy. As a result of this ignorance, panic is the initial response to disease. Later in life, awareness and comprehension have an effect on how people respond to diseases.

Chapter VI, Summation, summarises the thesis and the study's findings. Additionally, this chapter discusses the limitations of the study. This chapter puts forth the major findings of the study. The observations are listed and the inferences drawn are explained to aid comprehension.

Additionally, this chapter discusses a set of postulates that may aid in the pursuit of life satisfaction. This chapter also makes suggestions for future research on Garcia Marquez's works.

CHAPTER TWO

AN OVERVIEW OF THE THEORY

"The connection between psychology, mythology, and literature is as important as the connection between psychology and biology and the hard sciences." - Jordan Peterson

A theory is a rule that has been shaped as an endeavour to make sense of things that have previously been validated by information. It is utilized in the names of various standards acknowledged in established researchers, like the Big Bang Theory. Owing to the afflictions of trial and error and control, it is perceived to be bound to be valid than a speculation, which is a suspicion, a thought that is proposed for contention so it very well may be tried to check whether it very well may be valid. In the logical technique, the speculation is built before any relevant exploration has been finished, aside from an essential foundation survey. A hypothesis is generally provisional; it is a presumption or idea made stringently for the goal of being tested.

A theory is a connected arrangement of ideas and standards about a peculiarity, the reason for which is to make sense of or anticipate the peculiarity. Theories are fundamental in research for the accompanying reasons.

1. Theory gives ideas to name what is noticed and to make sense of connections between ideas. It permits to make sense of what is seen and to sort out some way to achieve change. It is an

instrument that empowers us to recognize an issue and to design a method for modifying what is going on.

2. Theory assists with legitimizing repayment to get financing and backing, the analyst needs to make sense of what is happening and prove its efficacy.
3. Theory assists with improving the development of the expert region to recognize a group of information with speculations from both inside and without the area of distance discovering that the collection of information develops with theory and deeper exploration. Accordingly, theory guides research.

The theory also helps us understand what we don't know and, therefore, is the only guide to research. Relating to theory, it increases its ability to solve other problems in different times and different places. (Moore, 1991)

Theories are continually re-examined as new information is found through research. With each new viewing as connected with the subject, speculations should be rebuilt and rethought. Three phases of hypothesis improvement in any new science are:

1. Speculative - endeavours to make sense of action.

2. Descriptive - accumulates illustrative information to portray what is truly occurring.

3. Constructive - modifies old hypotheses and grows new ones in view of proceeding with research.

The most common ways of creating theories are chiefly three. They are -

1. Theory-practice-theory - takes existing theory in training, apply to separate learning, foster new theory.
2. Practice-research-theory - sees what is going on in distance learning, submit to explore, foster theory from results.

3. Theory-theory-research/practice - expands on an underlying hypothesis to foster a subsequent theory, then apply and test it.

A theory has fluctuated capabilities, for example, -

1. To give general clarification to peculiarities - it is a definitive capability of a hypothesis where it makes sense of the design and elements of hierarchical life.
2. To direct exact exploration - by giving applied underpinnings to the advancement of speculation which are created to actually look at the proposed hypothetical clarifications with genuine reality.
3. To accommodate aggregate exploration - which accommodates the advancement of information by expanding upon prior research and by refining, reformulating, and expounding the theory.
4. To direct activity in the feeling of giving the premise of arriving at conclusions about commonsense ordinary inquiries - ideas and speculations empower the expert to get a handle on the intricacies of the real world and consequently accommodate vital and level-headed activity.

The significant parts of theory are idea, suspicion and speculation. Idea is a term that has been given a theoretical summed up importance. In organization, for example, like administration, casual association, and fulfillment are given summed up implications which by and by are utilized to depict conduct in reality. All in all, ideas are considerations, "Researchers, theorists and practitioners can agree on the meaning of such terms." (Reynold, 1971). Ideas being conceptual and general are guaranteed of their being free of any remarkable fleeting or spatial setting.

Assumption is an explanation that is acknowledged as obvious without evidence and without fundamentally being undeniable. This is on the grounds that a suspicion might be definitional in character; that is, it is a meaning of a given word.

Generalisation is an assertion or recommendation that shows the common relationship of at least two ideas. A speculation joins ideas in a significant style. Speculations are of four sorts, 1. assumptions, 2. theory, 3. principles and 4. laws.

Psychological Study

Psychology is the study of conduct and psyche. It incorporates the investigation of cognizant and oblivious peculiarities, as well as feeling and naturally suspected. It is a scholarly discipline of massive extension. Clinicians look for a comprehension of the new properties of cerebrums, and all the range of peculiarities connected to those rising properties, joining this way the more extensive neurological gathering of scientists. As a social science, it intends to comprehend people and gatherings by laying out broad standards and exploring explicit cases.

In this field, an expert professional or specialist is known as a clinician and can be delegated a social, conduct, or mental researcher. Analysts endeavour to figure out the job of mental capabilities in individual and social way of behaving, while likewise investigating the physiological and organic cycles that underlie mental capabilities and ways of behaving.

Clinicians investigate conduct and mental cycles, including insight, discernment, consideration, feeling, knowledge, emotional encounters, inspiration, working of the mind, and character. This stretches out to connection between individuals, like relational connections, including mental strength, family flexibility, and different regions. Clinicians of different directions additionally think about the oblivious brain. Clinicians utilize exact techniques to construe causal and corelational connections between psychosocial factors. Moreover, or in resistance, to utilizing experimental and rational strategies, some - particularly clinical and guiding clinicians - now and again depend upon representative translation and other inductive methods. Psychology has been portrayed as a hub science in that medication will in general draw mental exploration by means of neurology and psychiatry, while social sciences most regularly draw straightforwardly from subdisciplines inside psychology.

While knowledge in psychology is frequently applied to the appraisal and treatment of psychological well-being issues, it is likewise coordinated towards understanding and tackling issues in a few circles of human movement. By many records, the final intention of psychology is to serve the society. Most of analysts are associated with a helpful job of some sort, rehearsing in clinical, directing, or school settings. Many do logical examination on a large number of subjects connected with mental cycles and conduct, and commonly work in college brain science divisions or show in other scholarly settings (e.g., clinical schools, medical clinics). Some are utilized in modern and authoritative settings, or in different regions like human turn of events and maturing, sports, wellbeing, and the media, as well as in criminological examination and different parts of regulation.

There are various mental speculations that are utilized to make sense of and foresee a wide assortment of ways of behaving. One of the main things that another brain science understudy could see is that there are many theories to learn. Freud's psychoanalytic theory, Erikson's psychosocial theory, the Big Five theory, and Bandura's social learning theory are only a couple of models that could come into view.

These theories fill in various significant needs. There are three key motivations behind the existence of psychological theories.

1. They provide a basis for understanding the mind and behaviour - Theories give a system to figuring out human way of behaving, thought, and improvement. Having a wide base of understanding about the hows and whys of human way of behaving helps in grasping ourselves and other people better. Every theory gives a setting to grasp a specific part of human way of behaving. Social speculations, for instance, give a premise to understanding how individuals learn new things. From the perspective of these hypotheses, we can investigate a portion of the various ways that learning happens as well as the variables

that impact this kind of learning.

2. They inspire future research - Theories make a reason for future exploration. Scientists use speculations to frame theories that can then be tried. As new revelations are made and integrated into the first hypothesis, new inquiries and thoughts can then be investigated.
3. They can adapt and evolve - Theories are dynamic and continuously evolving. As new revelations are made, hypotheses are adjusted and adjusted to represent new data. While hypotheses are some of the time introduced as static and fixed, they will generally develop over the long run as new examination is investigated. Attachment theory, for instance, crafted by John Bowlby and Mary Ainsworth and has extended and developed to incorporate new portrayals of various connection styles.

Cognitive Dissonance Theory

Cognitive dissonance alludes to a circumstance including clashing perspectives, convictions or ways of behaving. This delivers a sensation of mental distress prompting a change in one of the perspectives, convictions or ways of behaving to diminish the uneasiness and re-establish harmony. For instance, when individuals smoke (conduct) and they know that smoking causes malignant growth (comprehension), they are in a condition of mental cacophony.

Cognitive Dissonance was first examined by Leon Festinger, emerging out of a member perception investigation of a faction that accepted that the earth would have been obliterated by a flood, and what happened to its individuals — especially the truly dedicated ones who had surrendered their homes and responsibilities to work for the clique — when the flood did not occur. While periphery individuals were more disposed to perceive that they had embarrassed themselves and to put it down to encounter, serious individuals were bound to re-decipher the proof to show that they were correct up and down (the earth was not obliterated in view of the unwavering nature of the clique individuals).

Festinger's (1957) cognitive dissonance theory proposes that we have an inward drive to hold every one of our perspectives and conduct as one and stay away from disharmony or discord. This is known as the guideline of mental consistency. At the point when there is an irregularity between mentalities or ways of behaving, something should change to kill the disharmony. It very well may be seen that disharmony hypothesis does not express that these methods of dissonance decrease will really work, just that people who are in a condition of mental discord will do whatever it takes to diminish the degree of their disharmony.

The theory of cognitive dissonance has been generally explored in various circumstances to foster the essential thought in more detail, and different variables that have been recognized which might be significant in disposition change. Common reasons for Cognitive Dissonance are:

1. Forced Compliance Behaviour - When somebody is compelled to openly accomplish something they secretly truly do not have any desire to do, cacophony is made between their cognizance and their way of behaving.

Forced Compliance happens when an individual plays out an activity that is conflicting with their convictions. The way of behaving cannot be changed, since it was at that point previously, so cacophony should be decreased by re-examining their mentality to what they have done. This forecast has been tried tentatively.

In a captivating examination, Festinger and Carlsmith (1959) requested members to play out a series from dull errands, (for example, turning stakes in a stake board for 60 minutes). As you can envision, member's mentalities toward this undertaking were

exceptionally negative. Festinger and Carlsmith (1959) explored in the event that causing individuals to play out a dull errand would make mental discord through constrained consistence conduct.

In their research facility explore, they involved 71 male pupils as members to play out a progression of dull errands, (for example, turning stakes in a stake board for 60 minutes).

They were then paid either $1 or $20 to tell a holding up member (a confederate) that the undertakings were truly fascinating. Practically every one of the members consented to stroll into the lounge area and convince the confederate that the exhausting examination would be entertaining.

At the point when the members were approached to assess the examination, the members who were paid just $1 evaluated the monotonous undertaking as more tomfoolery and agreeable than the members who were paid $20 to lie.

Being paid just $1 is not adequate motivator for lying thus the individuals who were paid $1 experienced disharmony. They could beat that cacophony by coming to accept that the assignments truly were intriguing and agreeable. Being paid $20 gives motivation to turning stakes, and there is thusly no dissonance.

2. Decision Making - Life is loaded up with choices, and choices (when in doubt) stir dissonance.

For instance, assume you needed to choose whether to acknowledge a task in a totally gorgeous region of the nation, or turn down the gig so you could be close to your loved ones. One way or another, you would encounter cacophony. Assuming that you accepted the position you would miss your friends and family; assuming that you turned the work down, you would long for the lovely streams, mountains, and valleys.

The two options have their valid statements and awful focuses. The rub is that going with a choice removes the likelihood that you can partake in the upsides of the rejected elective, yet it guarantees you that you should acknowledge the weaknesses of the picked other option.

Individuals have multiple ways of decreasing cacophony that is stirred by pursuing a choice (Festinger, 1964). One thing they can do is to change the way of behaving. As noted before, this is frequently extremely challenging, so individuals much of the time utilize different mental moves. A typical method for lessening cacophony is to build the engaging quality of the picked other option and to diminish the appeal of the dismissed other option. This is alluded to as "spreading apart the alternatives". Brehm (1956) was quick to research the connection among disharmony and direction.

Female members were educated they would assist in a review subsidized by a few makers. Members were likewise informed that they would get one of the items toward the finish of the examination to make up for their time and exertion.

The ladies then appraised the attractiveness of eight family items that went in cost from $15 to $30. The items incorporated a programmed espresso creator, an electric sandwich barbecue, a programmed toaster oven, and a versatile radio. Members in the benchmark group were basically given one of the items. Since these members did not settle on a choice, they had no discord to decrease. People in the low-discord bunch picked either an attractive item or another one with 3 point lesser value on a 8-point scale.

Members in the high-dissonance condition picked either a really attractive item or one evaluated only 1 point lower on the 8-point scale. In the wake of perusing the reports about the different items, people appraised the items once more. Members in the high-cacophony condition spread separated the choices fundamentally more than did the members in the other two circumstances.

At the end of the day, they were more probable than members in the other two circumstances to expand the engaging quality of the picked other option and to diminish the allure of the dismissed other option.

3. Effort - It likewise is by all accounts the case that we esteem most profoundly those objectives or things which have expected significant work to accomplish.

This is presumably in light of the fact that cacophony would be caused in the event that we burned through an extraordinary energy to accomplish something and, assessed it adversely. One could, obviously, burn through long stretches of energy into accomplishing something which ends up being a heap of trash and afterward, to stay away from the cacophony that produces, attempt to persuade themselves that they did not actually burn through long stretches of energy, or that the work was actually very pleasant, or that it was not exactly a great deal of exertion.

As a matter of fact, however, it appears one finds it simpler to convince ourselves that what they have accomplished is beneficial and that is what the majority of us do, assessing exceptionally something whose accomplishment has cost us dear - regardless of whether others think it is a lot of cop. This strategy for lessening disharmony is known as effort justification. If one puts in effort into an undertaking which we have decided to complete, and the errand turns out seriously, he/she experiences disharmony. To diminish this, he/she is spurred to attempt to feel that the errand ended up great.

An exemplary study of disharmony by Aronson and Mills (1959) shows the essential thought. The point of this trial was to explore the connection among disharmony and exertion.

Female understudies elected to partake in a conversation on the brain research of sex. In the 'gentle humiliation' condition, members read resoundingly to a male experimenter a rundown of sex-related words like 'virgin' and 'whore'.

In the 'serious humiliation' condition, they needed to peruse resoundingly revolting words and an exceptionally unequivocal sexual section. In the control condition, they went straight into the fundamental review. In all circumstances, they then heard an extremely exhausting conversation about sex in lower creatures. They were approached to rate how fascinating they had tracked down the conversation, and how fascinating they had found individuals associated with it. Members in the 'extreme humiliation' condition gave the best evaluating. It was seen that as assuming that an intentional encounter which has cost a great deal of exertion turns out seriously, disharmony is diminished by rethinking the experience as intriguing. This legitimizes the work made.

Settling Mental Disharmony

Dissonance can be decreased in one of three ways: 1. changing existing convictions,

2. adding new convictions, or 3. decreasing the significance of the convictions.

1. Change at least one of the perspectives, conduct, convictions, and so on, to make the connection between the two components a consonant one.

At the point when one of the discordant components is a specific way of behaving, the individual can change or dispose of the way of behaving. Notwithstanding, this method of disharmony decrease regularly presents issues for individuals, as it is frequently challenging for individuals to change all around scholarly conduct reactions (e.g., quitting any pretense of smoking).

2. Acquire new data that offsets the conflicting convictions.

For instance, figuring smoking causes cellular breakdown in the lungs will cause disharmony on the off chance that an individual smokes. In any case, new data, for example, research has not demonstrated most certainly that smoking causes cellular breakdown in the lungs may decrease the discord.

3. Reduce the significance of the perceptions (i.e., convictions, perspectives).

An individual could persuade himself/herself that it is smarter to enjoy every moment than to save for later. All in all, he could perceive himself that a short life loaded up with smoking and erotic delights is superior to a long life absent any and all such delights.

Along these lines, he would be diminishing the significance of the noisy discernment (smoking is bad for one's wellbeing).

Critique of Cognitive Dissonance Theory

There has been a lot of examination into Cognitive Dissonance, giving a few intriguing and in some cases startling discoveries. It is a hypothesis with exceptionally wide applications, showing that we go for the gold perspectives and ways of behaving, and may not utilize extremely sane strategies to accomplish it. It enjoys the benefit of being testable by logical means (i.e., tests). In any case, there is an issue according to a logical perspective, since we cannot truly notice cognitive dissonance, and thusly we cannot equitably gauge it (i.e., behaviourism). Thus, the term mental cacophony is to some degree emotional.

There is additionally some uncertainty (i.e., ambiguity) about the term 'disharmony' itself. Is it a discernment (as 'mental' proposes), or an inclination, or an inclination about an insight? Aronson's correction of the possibility of disharmony as an irregularity between an individual's self-idea and an insight about their conduct causes it to appear to be reasonable that discord is actually just culpability. There are additionally individual contrasts in whether individuals go about as this hypothesis predicts. Exceptionally restless individuals are bound to do as such. Many individuals appear to be ready to adapt to extensive cacophony and not experience the strains the hypothesis predicts.

At last, large numbers of the investigations supporting the hypothesis of mental disharmony have low natural legitimacy. For instance, turning stakes (as in Festinger's examination) is a fake undertaking that does not occur in regular day to day existence. Likewise, most of examinations involved understudies as members, which raise issues of a one-sided test.

Hope Theory

Charles Richard Snyder was an American clinician who spent significant time in positive psychology. He earned worldwide distinction for his work in clinical, social, character, and wellbeing brain science. His theories from the '80s and '90s connect with, in addition to other things, human reactions to individual criticism, human requirement for uniqueness, and the expectation thought process. In light of Snyder's work, more examinations were directed to connect expanded degrees of desire to scholastic and athletic execution and actual wellbeing and prosperity. By assisting individuals with turning out to be purported high-hopers, they gain a more inspirational perspective on life.

Three Components of Hope Theory

While discussing Snyder's Hope Theory, it is useful to initially characterize the word 'trust'. Hope should be visible as the apparent capacity to walk specific ways prompting an ideal objective. Furthermore, trust assists individuals with remaining propelled while strolling these ways. Trust comprises of both mental components and emotional components. Snyder's Hope Theory incorporates objectives, ways, and opportunity of decision. As indicated by him, there are no less than three parts that individuals can connect with trust, being:

1. the individual requirements to have centred contemplations,
2. the individual should foster techniques ahead of time to accomplish these objectives,
3. the individual must be spurred to put forth the attempt expected to arrive at these objectives in fact.

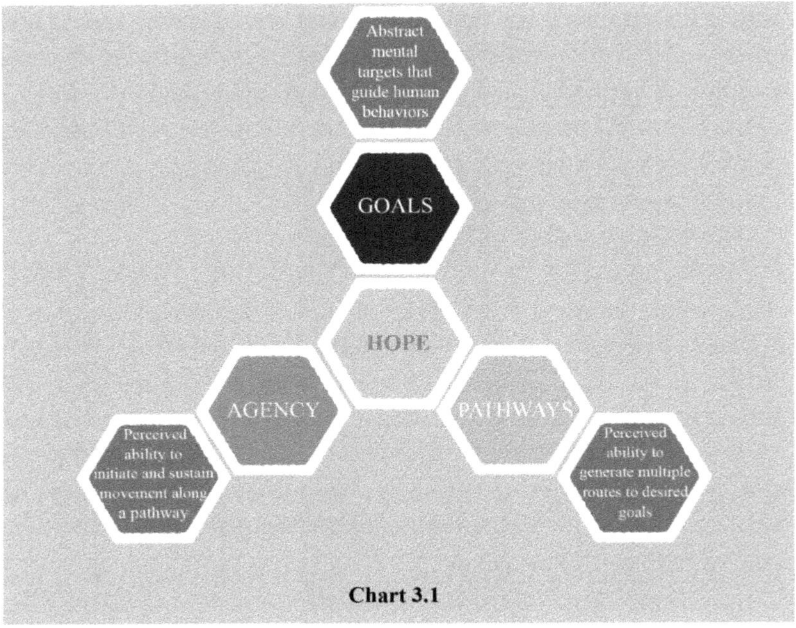

Chart 3.1

The more the individual has confidence in their own capacity to accomplish the parts recorded over, the more noteworthy is the opportunity that they will foster a sensation of trust.

Pathways and Agency Thinking

Objectives are conceptual and mental. They have the ability to direct human way of behaving. Snyder saw that quite a bit of human way of behaving is objective situated. Notwithstanding the recently referenced parts, Snyder's Hope Theory in this way recognizes two other significant elements that impact development towards the objective:

1. Pathways thinking

This is about the human capacity to produce various pathways from the present to the ideal future. Pathways centre around the apparent capacity to design various courses. This is about the mental capacity to deliver a pathway that prompts the objective, and to initially consider it.

2. Agency Thinking

This alludes to the degree of goal, certainty, and the human capacity to follow those various pathways to the ideal future as a matter of fact. The conviction and positive inspiration to follow the way is the key here. This is about full of feeling capacity.

Positive Emotions

The actual objectives additionally assume a significant part in Snyder's Hope Theory. Objectives that are important yet questionable are depicted as the anchors of Snyder's Hope Theory. They offer heading and guide you to the last objective. Boundaries can likewise assume a part. They might make it challenging to arrive at the objectives.

In the event that there is a boundary, a simple arrangement is stopped except if pathways believing is fortified to make another pathway.

Arriving at objectives will happen all the more effectively assuming feelings are good. By and large boundaries lead to gloomy feelings. By concocting new, elective pathways, the conviction and inspiration from office believing is reactivated, making it conceivable to arrive at the objective sooner. Obstructions are then viewed as difficulties, not long-lasting barricades. The key in Snyder's Hope Theory requires various pathways to an objective and the aim to adhere to those ways. It is about a repetitive connection among Pathways and Agency Thinking, with Pathways Thinking prompting more courses. The advancement of additional courses thusly prompts Agency Thinking and positive feelings.

To get a certain beginning in Snyder's Hope Theory, it assists with posing various inquiries, for example, 'What is happening?' and 'Where would I like to go?' and 'What is halting me?' These are normal Pathways Thinking questions. From Agency Thinking, you could pose inquiries, for example, 'Which qualities might I at any point use to accomplish my objective?', 'Which parts of my ongoing circumstance really benefit me?', and 'When was I fruitful in comparative circumstances before and why?'

When producing choices to arrive at the last objective, it is likewise useful to summon a strong idea that contains the conviction that you can genuinely make it happen. At the point when you do this, Pathways Thinking is presently not about various choices; it will likewise support Agency Thinking. This invigorates you, making it more probable that you will arrive at the objective.

Assessment Tools

Notwithstanding the Hope Theory, the American clinician likewise concocted an assessment apparatus. He created it to quantify trust. Concerning's Hope Theory, this turned into the Adult Dispositional Hope Scale (ADHS), planned to gauge trust in individuals more than fifteen years of age. It is a self-evaluation device. The assessment device comprises of a poll with twelve inquiries; six that pointed to Pathways Thinking and six that pointed to Agency Thinking. The Pathways questions are about the mental capacity to concoct inventive strides towards the objective. The Agency questions are about the full of feeling part of the cerebrum and the sense, inspiration, and conviction that individuals need to endeavour towards the objective.

Each question gives the respondent fill access a rating from 1 to 8 as per the Likert Scale; 1 demonstrates least acknowledgment, while 8 methods most acknowledgment with respect to the inquiry. The scale then, at that point, thinks of three scores; an expectation score zeroed in on Agency and Pathways questions together, and two separate scores for both. The absolute scores can change from 8 to 64. The higher the score, the more expectation an individual has.

Logical Inconsistencies to the Hope Theory

Snyder's expectation hypothesis has been scrutinized for overlooking ideas like self-adequacy and idealism (Lazarus, 1999, 2000; Peterson, 2000, 2006). Colon and Leaf (2002) contend against this absence of mix, as well as Snyder's (1994, 2002) accentuation on mental attributes over close to home qualities in his depiction of trust. One of their focal reactions is that the accentuation on individual organization clouds the social settings that shape insights and occasions. Snyder might contend, notwithstanding, that even in troublesome times, high-trust people's mental capital empowers them to observe elective ways to their objectives substantially more effectively (Snyder and Lopez, 2007). Colon and Leaf (2002) validate Snyder's model by expressing that an individual's expectation level is likewise impacted by others' evaluations. This was a thought for every one of the customers reviewed.

Likewise, Lazarus (1999, 2000) portrays trust as a survival technique, in light of the fact that without it, one would unavoidably encounter despair. Moreover, he causes qualms about trust's agentic esteem.

> "*erroneous as a result of 'we can/we will/we are able to' hope even after we are helpless to have an effect on the result. Self-efficacy, or a way of ability and management, facilitates hope, and it actually aids in mobilizing problem-focused cope actions, however it's not essential to hope (Lazarus, 1999).*"

According to Fredrickson, when a model incorporates an emotive component, it increases hope by assisting shoppers in developing positive emotions and thus broadening their "thought-action repertoire, suppressing negative emotions, and increasing resilience" (2001). It is easy to envision how a shopper could feel more confident in those conditions.

Averill et al. (1990) recently fostered a diagram of trust that incorporated different unmistakable parts. People trust in trust when they accept their ideal result is both feasible and socially and ethically fine.

Likewise with Snyder's model, confident people make a move to achieve their objectives. Bruninink and Malle's resulting exploratory review (2005) looked to lay out a differentiation between these two focal ideas. As per their discoveries, members in their review referenced trust for of "keeping someone focused on their goals, keeping them going, or regulating negative emotions"

(2005). Their discoveries characterized trust as "an emotion felt by an individual when he or she is focused on a significant positive future outcome", oftentimes with little command over the result and regularly with very little administration over the result (2005). Consequently, this study recognizes trust from elective states, and, in opposition to Snyder's mental component model, members characterized trust in close to home terms, while they characterize confidence as a mental element idea. While Snyder and elective scientists share a few likenesses, for example, members' acknowledgment of the differentiation among trust and good faith, elective specialists examine trust as a subset of hopefulness or self-viability as opposed to as an unmistakable idea.

Carver and Scheier (2002), two trailblazers in the field of idealism, contend that there is areas of strength for a between Snyder's expectation hypothesis (1994) and their meaning of positive thinking. Moreover, they raise doubt about Snyder's model's accentuation on confidential office. They contend that having confidence in a positive result is undeniably more significant than including a feeling of organization inside the cycle. For instance, they declare that non-strict people might give up private command over occasions for help from above. In this way, people with non-common convictions experienced less despondency and further developed wellbeing, as per the examination. In any case,

> "*the people who attest that basic qualifications exist among good faith and trust, most eminently with regards to organization - in addition to the need yet additionally the means by which (Snyder et al. 2000; Gallagher and Lopez, 2009; Rand and Cheavens, 2009).*"

Conclusion

The theories and ideas mentioned in this chapter lays down the framework within which this study proceeds. Cognitive Dissonance Theory and Hope Theory are used in the further chapters to achieve the objectives of the study. Being a psychological study aimed at analysing the thinking and behavioural aspects of the major characters in the selected works, theoretical insight and scientific explanations are drawn from these theories.

Cognitive Dissonance Theory propounds that an inner drive exists within every individual that rationalises and justifies to oneself their actions. Through this, the person is able to maintain the harmony between his/her beliefs and actions. Individualism, which is a major aspect under examination, is directly related to Cognitive Dissonance, wherein a person's individualistic behaviour may often defer from social precedents. As such, this theory is used in this study to analyse the individualistic behaviour of major characters in the selected works.

Hope Theory points out that the more the individual hopes the greater is the chance that they achieve their goals. Hope is the positive emotion that keeps an individual go in their desired direction. Therefore, this theory has been used in study to analyse the theme of hope and the lack of it, which are prominent themes in the works of Garcia Marquez.

CHAPTER THREE

INDIVIDUALISM: A PATH TO HAPPINESS

"If a man is not faithful to his own individuality, he cannot be loyal to anything." - Claude McKay

Introduction

ndividualism may be termed as the moral standpoint, political philosophy, ideology or social outlook that focuses on the mores and values of an individual. An individualist believes in practicing and pursuing one's aims and wishes; thus, values self-dependence and freedom, encourages individuals to give precedence to their own interests rather than giving into societal norms and simultaneously oppose any external force that resists their goals, be it the society or the government. Its contrast from terms, such as totalitarianism and collectivism, is quite frequently used as the general definition of individualism.

The individual is the centre of individualism and its fundamental premise is that in the struggle for emancipation the primary significance is for the human individual. The movements such as anarchism, existentialism and liberalism consider the individual as their focal point. An individual's right to freedom and self-actualisation is also an aspect of individualism.

Since long, the term individualism has been used to denote the state of being an individual, individuality, or possessing a unique personal quality or trait. Creative and Bohemian pursuits and lifestyles, where self-creation and innovativeness prevail over popular styles and traditional ways such as humanist disposition, are also included in individualism.

Although it is widely believed that the word individualism was introduced to the English language first by Utopian socialists as a derogatory term, there is also the possibility of them being influenced by Saint-Simonianism. It was through the writings of the millenarian and Christian Israelite, James Elishama Smith that the term gained positive connotation in Britain. He was one for the initial followers of Robert Owen but later he gave up its collective idea of property in favour of individualism which according to him encouraged original genius as it was founded in universalism. He argued that only through individualism can an individual amass wealth and improve their state of happiness and it was impossible otherwise. In his1847 work *Elements of Individualism,* the Unitarian preacher by name William Maccall, who is possibly a friend of Smith and believed to be highly inspired by German Romanticism, Thomas Carlyle and John S Mill, gradually concluded positively.

An individual is a person or a characteristic that is unique within a collection. Individual is a term that dates all the way back to the fifteenth century and is still used today in disciplines such as Statistics and Metaphysics to refer to something that cannot be further divided, usually referring to any numerically singular thing, though it can also refer to someone, as in the problem of proper nouns. Individualism, which dates all the way back to the seventeenth century, demonstrates uniqueness and distinction. Individuality is the condition or state of being a unique or distinct person; someone who is distinct from the rest with unique characteristics as a result of possessing his or her own desires, goals, and aspirations that are distinct from those of others.

Individuation principle

Individuation principle, also known as the principium individuation, describes the process by which a thing is distinguished from other things. Following Carl Gustav Jung's theory of individuation, individuation is defined as the process by which the individual and collective unconscious are brought into consciousness through methods such as dreams, active imagination, or free association in order to be assimilated into the whole personality. Psyche integration is an entirely natural process that must take place in order for it to be successful. In Jung's view, the process of individualization is the most important stage in human development. With the publication of *L'individuation Psychique Et Collective*, Gilbert Simondon developed a theory of individual and collective individuation in which the individual subject is regarded as an effect rather than a cause of individuation. An infinitely differentiating ontological process thus takes the place of the individual atom. Identification is a process that is perpetually incomplete and always leaves behind a "pre-individual" that facilitates the emergence of new individuals in the future. Sigmund Freud's ideas on individuation, as well as those of Friedrich Nietzsche and Bernard Stiegler, are all referenced and modified in Bernard Stiegler's philosophy. For Stiegler,

> "*the I, as a psychic individual, can only be thought in relationship to we, which is a collective individual. The I is constituted in adopting a collective tradition, which it inherits and in which a plurality of I's acknowledge each other's existence.(2004)*"

Chart 4.1 illustrates the concept of individualism. Every individual has two circles around him/her. Each circle has its own significance. These circles can be termed as intellectual or ideological spaces. The first circle or the inner circle is where the individual stands and his/her ideas and beliefs are predominant. The second circle or the outer circle is where the external ideas and beliefs lie, which are the major social forces such as family, society, religion, culture, government and economical factors. Between these two circles lies a buffer space which can be termed as the transitional space. This is where the personal beliefs and ideas mingle with the external ideas and beliefs to reach a compromise to satisfy both parties involved. As long as the individual practices his/her own ideas, they could be called individualists.

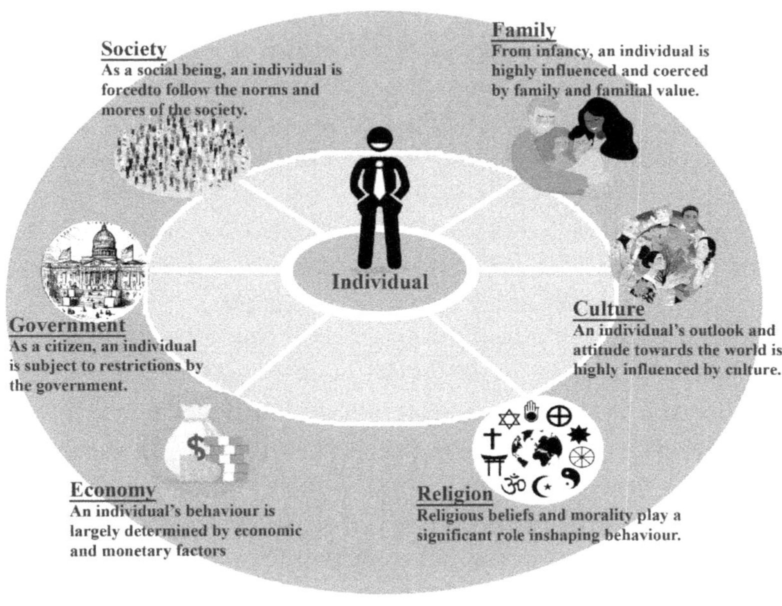

Chart 4.1

Factors Influencing Individualism

The outer circle constantly exerts pressure upon the transitional space and in turn on the inner circle, as a means of making the individual conform to the socially accepted behaviour. This pressure at times succeeds in crumpling the inner circle and causing the person to lose his/her individuality and behave strictly according to the expectation of the external forces. While at other times it generates a greater force within the individual, which causes the inner circle to push back and expand, resulting in high individualism. Such persons behave quite differently from the general population, exhibit unique behavioural traits and often harbour controversial beliefs.

Individualism and Cognitive Dissonance

Cognitive dissonance is a psychological term that refers to when a person holds contradictory beliefs, ideas, or values. It is typically experienced as psychological stress when a person engages in behaviour that is in violation of one or more of these beliefs, ideas, or values. According to this theory, when two actions or ideas are psychologically incompatible, people will go to any length to make them psychologically compatible.

People experience discomfort when their beliefs conflict with new information they have learned. They then attempt to resolve the conflict in order to alleviate their discomfort.

In *A Theory of Cognitive Dissonance* (1957), Leon Festinger proposed that human beings strive for internal psychological consistency in order to be able to function mentally in the real world. When a person is confronted with internal inconsistency, he or she becomes psychologically uneasy and motivated to find a solution to the cognitive dissonance that has been created. To justify stressful behaviour, they frequently alter their cognition, either by adding new components to the cognition that cause psychological dissonance or by avoiding situations and contradictory information that would exacerbate the cognitive dissonance.

It takes a lot of mental energy to try to bring two opposing ideas or experiences together. Being able to sit with those seemingly contradictory statements that all appear to be true takes time and effort on your part. Theoretically, according to Festinger, certain individuals would inevitably resolve cognitive dissonance by blindly believing whatever they desired.

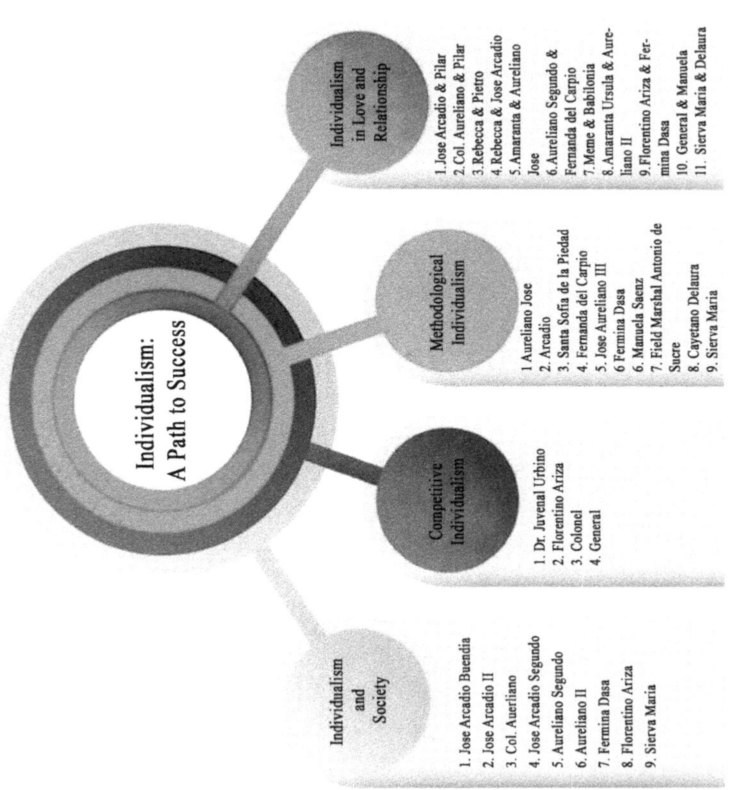

Chart 4.2

Characters Displaying Individualism

Individualism and Society

Individualism maintains that an individual participating in the public sphere seeks to learn and discover their own advantages on an individual basis, without regard for the cultural design's interests (a nonconformist need not be a vain person). The individual does not adhere to a single mode of thought, but rather creates a synthesis of several, based on his or her own interests and particularly the viewpoints that are useful to him or her. On a cultural level, the nonconformist is a member of an organised political and moral ground in the distant future. A characteristic of a nonconformist is autonomous reasoning and assessment. According to Jean-Jacques Rousseau, his concept of general will in *The Social Contract* (1762) is not a collection of individual wills but rather serves the individual's interests. The limitation of law itself would benefit the individual, as disregard for the law essentially entails, in Rousseau's view, a type of obliviousness and accommodation to one's own interests rather than the favoured self-rule of reason.

Individualism versus community is a typical division in diverse examination. Worldwide similar investigations have tracked down that the world's societies shift in how much they underline singular self-sufficiency, opportunity and activity (individualistic characteristics), separate adjustment to bunch standards, keeping up customs and dutifulness to in-bunch authority (collectivistic qualities). Individualism and community are social dichotomies in terms of degree, not type. Individualism on a social level is inextricably linked to per capita GDP. The lifestyles of economically developed regions such as Western Europe, Japan, North America, and Australia are among the most individualistic on the planet. Eastern Europe, South America, and East Asia's territories, for example, have societies that are neither excessively individualistic nor excessively collectivist. The world's most collectivistic societies are found in economically developing regions such as Sub-Saharan Africa, the Middle East and Northern Africa, Central Asia, Central America, and South and Southeast Asia.

Ruth Benedict previously demonstrated in her book *The Chrysanthemum and the Sword* that social orders and gatherings can differ in their reliance on predominantly “self-in-relation-to” (1946) (individualistic, and additionally self-interested) practises rather than “other-in-relation-to” (bunch-based, and group- or society-disapproved) practises. She distinguished between “blame” (ibid) social orders (for example, middle age Europe) with a “inward reference standard” (ibid) and “disgrace” (ibid) social orders (for example, Japan, bringing disgrace upon one’s forefathers) with a “outer reference standard” (ibid), in which individuals seek criticism from their companions regarding whether an activity is “worthy” (ibid) or not.

Individualism is frequently contrasted with despotism or with cooperation, but there is a spectrum of cultural practises ranging from profoundly individualistic social orders to blended social orders to collectivist social orders. Garcia Marquez’s characters frequently stand apart from their peers. Their behaviour and life choices frequently garner the society’s attention.

In *One Hundred Years of Solitude*, Jose Arcadio Buendia, the patriarch of the Buendia clan, was every bit the individualist one can hope to be. He has his own way of doing anything. He was greatly innovative and came up with creative ways of dealing with things. His personal quirks though innovative often bordered on eccentricity and insanity. Starting with his marriage to Ursula Iguaran to his sad final days bound to a tree, everything was unique in his own ways. His marriage was against the social norms as he was related to Ursula by blood.

There existed the superstition that the offspring of such a relation would be born deformed, that is, with a pigtail. Yet, he married Ursula and lived a long life with her. Fearing the superstition Ursula initially wore a chastity belt to prevent the consummation of their marriage and the consequent birth of a deformed child. But, he later asks her to abandon the belt and consummate the marriage after he killed a man who humiliated him for not having consummated his marriage. Thus, he overcame the external pressure of the superstition on his marriage.

> "*Jose Arcadio Buendia went into the bedroom as his wife was putting on her chastity pants. Pointing the spear at her he ordered:*
>
> *"Take them off." Úrsula had no doubt about her husband's decision. "You'll be responsible for what happens," she murmured. Jose Arcadio Buendía stuck the spear into the dirt floor.*
>
> *"If you bear iguanas, we'll raise iguanas," he said. "But there'll be no more killings in this town because of you." (OHYS 22)*"

In this case, it can be found that he encountered cognitive dissonance which he overcame by being bold enough to accept the consequences of his actions. He felt the blow on his self-esteem and the guilt hard and decided that such an incident should never happen again. He took measures to ensure the same and it was effective in keeping the social order but the guilt was with him throughout in the form of the ghost of the dead man.

Jose Arcadio II is the eldest son of Jose Arcadio and Ursula Buendia. He was conceived and born before the founding of Macondo, which makes him the first member of the Macondo family. Even though he does not have the same level of imagination as his younger brother, he does share the same level of passion and machismo as the Colonel. Ursula's long-dormant fears about his sexual development are reawakened by his prodigious sexual development when he is fourteen. Eventually, Jose Arcadio II falls in love with Pilar Ternera, a fortune teller in the town of Macondo. He is drawn to her by the "smell of smoke" (*OHYS* 26) that he detects under her armpits and on her skin. The affair between Jose Arcadio II and Pilar Ternera quickly leads to predictable consequences. Nevertheless, the news that Pilar Ternera has given birth to his child has scared and depressed him to the point where he flees wearing "a red cloth around his head" (*OHYS*34), with the help of a gypsy girl and her people.

Jose Arcadio II returned to Macondo as a fully matured man. He had circumnavigated the globe sixty-five times and considers himself to be a member of "a crew of sailors without a country" (*OHYS* 93). All the women of Macondo were captivated by his colossal physical stature and fantastic tales of adventure in an incredible way. The handsome Jose Arcadio II usurped Pietro Crespi in the affections of Rebecca, his step-sister, after ploughing through the beautiful women of Macondo with a broad swath of his sword. After brutally breaking Pietro Crespi's engagement, Jose Arcadio II marries Rebeca. The union is legalised, much to Ursula's dismay, but Father Nicanor reveals in a Sunday sermon that the couple were not actually brother and sister, as he had assumed. Ursula, on the other hand, forbids them from ever returning to the family home.

A few years after his father's death, Jose Arcadio II settles into a home built by his son Arcadio and takes on the role of feudal lord. He uses coercion to seize the best plots of land surrounding Macondo, and he taxes peasants "every Saturday with his hunting dogs and double-barrelled shotgun" (*OHYS* 117) on the grounds that Macondo's land was improperly distributed by his father, who was insane. During one particularly dramatic episode, after saving his brother from a firing squad, he takes on the persona of a heroic tyrant.

> "*When the squad took aim, the rage had materialized into a viscous and bitter substance that put his tongue to sleep and made him close his eyes. Then the aluminum glow of dawn disappeared and he saw himself again in short pants, wearing a tie around his neck, and he saw his father leading him into the tent on a splendid afternoon, and he saw the ice. When he heard the shout he thought that it was the final command to the squad.*
>
> *He opened his eyes with a shudder of curiosity, expecting to meet the incandescent trajectory of the bullets, but he only*

saw Captain Roque Carnicero with his arms in the air and Jose Arcadio crossing the street with his fearsome shotgun ready to go off. (OHYS 132)"

These above instances are testaments to the individuality demonstrated by Jose Arcadio. Each of his life's choices was heavily in contrast with the social norms and customs. Yet, nothing seemed to bother him in his pursuit of life. As a teenager, he first found himself in conflict with the norms of the society and it caused him to runaway due to his lack of experience in life. But, upon his return from exile, he is a well experienced and well travelled man. He had seen enough of the world to know that nothing else mattered when it comes to personal fulfilment. As a result, he is highly individualistic and rarely encounters cognitive dissonance. The instance of him saving the Colonel from the firing squad even at the peril of his life could easily be one of the rarest moments where he faced dissonance. But, his confidence in his intimidating physical appearance and strength was more than enough to overcome the situation.

Colonel Aureliano Buendia, the second child of Jose Arcadio Buendia and Ursula Iguaran, is a well-known revolutionary leader who commands the Liberal armed forces throughout the country. Meanwhile, he is the novel's most prominent craftsman figure, having performed multiple roles as a writer, a skilled silversmith, and the creator of numerous exquisitely detailed brilliant fish. However, Aureliano's (I) inability to deal with intense emotion contributes to his extraordinary fight balance and creative ability; however, Marquez's depiction of the Colonel melting his golden fishes "he kept on making two fishes a day and when he finished twenty-five he would melt them down and start all over again." (*OHYS* 270) and restarting from the beginning indicates that this balance and centre are not worth the price they have been paid.

Aureliano (I) is unmoved by anyone or anything, and he never shows genuine emotion. Remedios Moscote, his child wife at the time, appears to have a profound effect on him right from the start.

Nonetheless, he discovers that his grief is not nearly as significant as he had anticipated when she passes away unexpectedly. During the conflict, he reveals himself to be much more solidified to emotion, and, as a result, his memory and every one of his sentiments are gradually eroded until they are completely gone. He has consumed the entirety of his sonnets and, before the end of his life, he has decided to stop creating new brilliant fish. After all is said and done, he makes twenty-five of them and then softens them down, repurposing the metal for the following cluster. In this vein, he lives exclusively in the present, acknowledging that time moves in cycles and that the present is all that exists for a man like him, who has no recollections of the past.

The suicide attempt of Colonel Aureliano Buendia demonstrates how profound his despondency has reached the point at which he realises that common conflict is pointless and that pride is the only thing keeping the various factions fighting. At the same time, his frustration is a powerful critique of the sadness that results from a lack of direction, as well as a critique of the worthlessness that results from a lack of direction. Colonel Aureliano encountered cognitive dissonance when he had to stop fighting at the behest of the other rebel leaders who accepted the peace. He knew deep inside that they still had a chance to win but his comrades had lost their morale. Therefore, he understood the futility of his pursuit and laid down his arms. Yet, in his heart of hearts he kept the flame of revolution ablaze. His mental unrest at the undesirable happenings in Macondo is visible when he expresses his desire to arm his seventeen sons and restart the rebellion.

The family's lineage is carried on to the fourth generation by the twin sons and daughter of Arcadio and Santa Sofia. Jose Arcadio Segundo is the younger of the twin children of Arcadio and Santa Sofia de la Piedad. It is possible that Jose Arcadio Segundo was exchanged for his twin brother, Aureliano Segundo, at the time of his birth. When Jose Arcadio Segundo is young, he witnesses an execution and develops into a frail, hard- working man who is singularly focused and becoming increasingly academic, much like his grandfather Colonel Aureliano Buendia. As a cockfighter and a stray, he discovers a purpose in life while leading the strikers against the banana organisation. After the strikers' massacre, he isolates himself in Melquiades' old study-room, attempting to interpret the ancient prophecies and preserving the memory of the slaughter. When he discovers that no one believes the slaughter occurred, he decides to resurrect Melquiades' old research. "Jose Arcadio Segundo dedicated himself then to peruse the manuscripts of Melquiades many times, and with so much more pleasure when he could not understand them." (*OHYS* 318)

Jose Arcadio Segundo faces cognitive dissonance when he fails in his attempt to remind the residents Macondo about the banana massacre. He is aware of his duty as the sole survivor and witness of the massacre but when he is unable to convince the people he stops trying. The spirit of enquiry and thirst for truth is his unique feature but he falls deep into himself and gives up on the society. He, then, focuses on his own enquiries which become his sole purpose for existence.

Aureliano (II) is the ill-conceived child of Meme and Mauricio Babilonia. His scandalised grandmother, Fernanda del Carpio, disguises him as Aureliano (II). He grows up in the Buendia family as a recluse, gradually acclimating to society. Aureliano (II) evolves into a researcher, and it is he who ultimately translates Melquiades' predictions. He fathers the child Aureliano (III) with his aunt, Amaranta Ursula, who dies shortly after birth. Aureliano (II) displays offensive conduct because of his obliviousness of the external world. When he can encounter the world, he deals with it and attempts to adjust to it however but he finds out the fate that anticipates him and Macondo. He does not attempt to defeat it. He acknowledges the looming debacle.

Before reaching the final line, however, he had already understood that he would never leave that room, for it was foreseen that the city of mirrors (or mirages) would be wiped out by the wind and exiled from the memory of men at the precise moment when Aureliano Babilonia would finish deciphering the parchments, and that everything written on them was unrepeatable since time immemorial and forever more, because races condemned to one hundred years of solitude did not have a second opportunity on earth. (*OHYS* 422)

Aureliano Babilonia initially faces cognitive dissonance at encounter with the wider society. He has no experience in dealing with the society. When he gets an opportunity to face the world, he is overwhelmed at the freedom that he is bestowed.

He tries to make to most out of it, even at the cost of forgetting his obligation as a father. His actions lead to the death of his offspring and this leads him down the path of desolation and guilt. He thus retreats from the society and back to his home. There he discovers the fate that awaits him and Macondo. Here, he further faces dissonance, that is, he gives up on his primal instinct of survival. He does not make use of his knowledge about the impending disaster and embraces death.

In *Love in the Time of Cholera,* social norms are violated quite a number of times by most of the major characters. To point out a few instances, the marriage between Fermina and Dr. Urbino, the late blossoming of widowed Fermina's and Florentino's relationship and a vast majority of Florentino's sexual escapades were blatant violation of societal norms. These characters gave preference to their own choices rather than the whims and fancies of people surrounding them.

By accepting the proposal of Dr. Urbino, Fermina exercised her right to overcome the barriers of social class imposed over her. Her decision to marry Dr. Urbino was in fact her protest against those people who wrote her threatening and abusive letters anonymously.

Initially, she was against the marriage but when she was pressurised to step back, she decided against her previous desires. She asserted herself and became the wife of

Dr. Urbino and the daughter-in-law of a prestigious household. It is evident that she encountered cognitive dissonance in this decision. But, she was able to overcome it through her need to prove to the world that she was indeed in great fit in the class to which others tried to deny her entry.

When it comes to the case of the late blossoming of the relationship between Florentino and Fermina, they both stood their ground against social norms and the dogma of old-age love. It was Fermina's daughter who first hinted her disapproval of Fermina's occasional meetings with Florentino. She was furious upon hearing the allegations of her daughter and took measures to keep her in line. She had her own reservations against a relationship with Florentino after the death of her husband, but gradually she was convinced by the persuasive letters of Florentino. She then accepted to join him on a cruise in the river boat.

> "*"What I would like is to walk out of this house, and keep going, going, going, and never come back," she said.*
>
> *"Take a boat," said Florentino Ariza. Fermina Daza looked at him thoughtfully.*
>
> *"Well, I might just do that," she said. (LTC 324-325)*"

When the boat reached the final destination, she came to her senses and refused to be seen with Florentino in the public. Yet, she chose to be with him rather than give in to societal pressure.

> "*The party was over: among them she saw many faces she knew, some of them friends who until a short while ago had attended her in her grief, and she rushed to take refuge in her cabin. Florentino Ariza found her there, distraught: she would rather die than be seen on a pleasure trip, by people she knew, so soon after the death of her husband. Her preoccupation affected Florentino Ariza so much that he promised to think of some way to protect her other than keeping her in the cabin. (LTC 342)*"

Fermina goes through cognitive dissonance at various phases in the relationship due to social pressure and morals. But, it was through her unique ways that she faced those situations. She was able to convince herself that she deserved to live a happy life even as a widow. The strong emotional support and motivation given by Florentino was another factor that enabled her to overcome the dissonance.

Florentino Ariza was born as an illegitimate child and lived his young years bearing the stigma. He rose to a position of wealth and respect in his later years with the support of his uncle Don Leo. Yet, as a man of age and still being unmarried he was looked upon with suspicion by the society. There were even rumours of him being secretly gay and having relationships with young boys that he picked up around the town. All his life, he lived against the social norms, indulging in secret affairs with hundreds of women while remaining loyal to his one true love. This is a matter of contention, as being loyal to a lover typically involves staying away from physical or emotional relationship with others. Yet, his actions may be justified as a means of escaping the pain he endured due to his separation from Fermina. Finally, after the death of Dr. Urbino, he rekindles his relationship with Fermina and breaks up with fourteen year old America Vicuna. He tells her that he is getting married. She is shocked and astonished in disbelief.

> "*Still looking at her, he said without warning:*
>
> *"I am going to marry."*
>
> *She looked into his eyes with a flash of uncertainty, her spoon suspended in midair, but then she recovered and smiled.*
>
> *"That's a lie," she said. "Old men don't marry."(LTC 289)*"

Dr. Juvenal Urbino del Calle is the city's most educated and most well-known individual. Urbino is an apathetic, close-mouthed man, but he is not heartless. He marries Fermina on the grounds that he admires her haughty, genuine manner. He devotes more time to his pet parrot than to his two children. His aloofness may stem from his affluent upbringing, in contrast to Florentino, who is a labourer. He is a legitimate man, motivated by a strong faith in God, and he suffers when he is unable to resist the allures of Barbara Lynch, with whom he undermines his better half. He is relieved when Fermina discovers his undermining her, as the immense guilt he feels prevents him from getting a charge out of the joy he once took in disclosing his 'moral infringement' against Barbara.

In the above characters, one can see the contrasting traits that make them members of the society yet simultaneously set them apart. Their behaviours, beliefs and attitudes are quite different from the society they live in. While Dr. Urbino is a true social being bent on bettering his society, he does hold a unique temperament and distinctive behaviour from the rest of his society, whereas Florentino is indifferent to the society.

Sierva Maria is the daughter of the Marquis in the novel *OfLoveandOtherDemons*. She was neglected by her parents and raised by the slaves of the household. Therefore she gets both a Christian and Yoruba upbringing. This becomes her individuality and becomes the reason for her doom. She speaks African dialects and wears stone necklaces. Her behaviour and way of life was primarily African while she was of the Aristocratic class. This is seen as an abomination by the Church and the society. But, she continues to stay the same way. It was as if she was not of that world. "It is not that the girl is unfit for everything, it is that she is not of this world." (*OLOD, 46*)

In the case of Sierva Maria, she seems to face no cognitive dissonance as her cognition is quite different from that of anybody else. Her upbringing was through a blend of cultures which causes her to be inclusive of all cultures and cultural traits. She lived her life as per her choice and that was not acceptable to the society. They institutionalise and incarcerate her. Had she given up her beliefs and way of life, she could have lived on but that kind of life could not be counted as living. Therefore, she holds on to her ways and embraces her destiny.

Competitive Individualism

According to Oxford Dictionary, "competitive individualism" in sociology is "the view that achievement and non-achievement should depend on merit". Effort and ability are viewed as necessary conditions for success. Competition is viewed as a legitimate method of allocating scarce resources and rewards. Accepting the competitive individualism perspective fosters a winning culture and the belief that competition brings out the best in people.

Competitive individualism is a subtype of individualism that develops as a result of competitive systems. The system's purpose is to perpetuate inequality in society and in fields of human engagement. This attribute the ups and downs of a person's life to themselves by ignoring a variety of factors such as socioeconomic class, race, and gender, to name a few. It bolsters privilege theories, which assert the superiority of certain individuals over others in the hierarchy of ranks. Cooperation is considered to be a more effective means of achieving greater individuality.

Dr. Urbino, in *Love in the Time of Cholera*, is completely indifferent, enjoying little more than chess, medication, and unfamiliar books. He is an older gentleman who continues to make house decisions for his patients, despite the fact that he has examined the most recent clinical advancements in Europe. Despite his commanding public presence, he is a frail, fainthearted man at home. When Fermina requests that he confront his mother with dignity, he is too terrified to do so. He surrenders his pride and submits to his significant other once more following a domestic conflict with Fermina in which he was genuinely and truly right. He is both admirable and pitiable, even more so when he is weakened by his mature age.

Though the doctor is submissive before his wife and mother at most times, his prowess in his profession is unquestionable. He almost single-handedly saves the city from the cholera pandemic and it is under his suggestion that the city council looks into the sanitation facilities in the slum areas and introduces tremendous reforms in the infrastructure. Dr. Urbino seems to care only for his public reputation and professional life as it is the only sphere where he strives for his beliefs. When in conflict with his wife or mother he always chose to give up without a fight even when he knew he was right, as he found it futile to continue the argument.

Florentino Ariza is another character who exhibits competitive individualism. He initially belonged to an economically and socially weak family. While meeting Fermina for the first time, he was just a mail-boy in the telegraph office. But, later when his love is rebuffed and Fermina marries the doctor who belonged to the upper class of the society and was socially well admired for his success, he vows to himself that he would become successful and wealthy so that he could be worthy of Fermina. As time progresses, Florentino could be seen climbing the ladders of success and acquiring social status. It is his determination and deep desire for Fermina that makes him capable of achieving this feat. Unlike any other person who would wish to be successful for his/her own sake, Florentino does it for a purpose which seems futile. He displays cognitive dissonance in this aspect where he seriously believes that he would be able to win back the affection of Fermina if he becomes financially successful.

In *No One Writes to the Colonel*, the colonel is not just the hero of the novel, he is the novel, for it is his humour and incongruity, his pride and fortitude against the odd misfortune of destitution and political restraint, that give the novel poise and design. This insightful yet innocent man expects such a dramatic height throughout the story. In spite of the fact that he goes to sit tight for the mail boat each Friday with confident assumption, his surrendered reaction is consistently something very similar: "No one writes to the Colonel." (*NWC* 22) Although he is regularly self-destroying, accommodated to the severe system which controls his life, he keeps up his pride. For instance, he does not wear a cap thus, as he says, "I won't have to take it off for anyone." (*NWC* 52)

He is both hopeful and amusing, a blend that makes him significant in contemporary fiction. At the point when his significant other says that he is just quite emaciated, he answers that he is dealing with himself so he can sell himself: "I've already been hired by a clarinet factory." (*NWC* 31) When his better half mourns that the mush they are eating is from corn left over from the chicken, and says, "'That's right.' The Colonel sighed, 'Life is the best thing that's ever been invented.'" (*NWC* 42) Albeit the Colonel has nothing so exceptionally substantial with which to battle, he is no less an illustration of a man who supports 'beauty under tension'.

The General in His Labyrinth starts with Simon Bolivar, otherwise called "the General," preparing to leave Colombia for Europe. Garcia Marquez shows a more human, defective side of Bolivar than is normally seen, and this portrayal got a blended reaction. Bolivar leaves Colombia, venturing to every part of the Magdalena River, and clearly he is breaking down. His well-being is poor, and he is not just about as loved as he used to be. During his excursion, he gets together with an old companion, is halted by police (at that point, when they accept he is as yet the president, they commend him), and learns of the commotion of the public authority he has given up. This is decimating to him and fills him with a feeling of worthlessness. Ultimately, he passes on, his endeavour to go to Europe having fizzled.

It could be said that the General was competing with himself and the entire nation to emerge as the most honourable and noble human being when he gives up his position as the President of Gran Colombia. In his attempt to be the better human being, he exhibited high individualism and while deeply hoping that the people would call him back. He was adamant in his decision that, even when he knew that the people needed him; he did not forgo his decision. "Life had already given him sufficient reasons for knowing that no defeat was the final one." (*GHL* 48)

Methodological Individualism

Methodological individualism as a method is the belief that phenomena can only be understood through an examination of how they are caused by the motivations and actions of individual agents. Economic theory explains human behaviour in terms of rational choices constrained by prices and incomes. Individual preferences are taken for granted by the economist. Becker and Stigler make a compelling case for this position:

> *"On the traditional view, an explanation of economic phenomena that reaches a difference in tastes between people or times is the terminus of the argument: the problem is abandoned at this point to whoever studies and explains tastes (psychologists? anthropologists? phrenologists? sociobiologists?). On our preferred interpretation, one never reaches this impasse: the economist continues to search for differences in prices or incomes to explain any differences or changes in behaviour. (1977)"*

The third era Buendias from *OneHundredYearsofSolitude*are not far away from the eccentricities of their precursors. They display a reasonable amount of disharmony, but their individualism is more methodological than societal. The third era individuals are each the children of Jose Arcadio and Colonel Aureliano.

Colonel Aureliano Buendia and Pilar Ternera have a son named Aureliano Jose. Aureliano Jose becomes obsessed with his aunt, Amaranta, and follows in his father's footsteps by joining the liberal army after she completes the undertaking. Despite the fact that he abandons the military to return to her, she dismisses him, shocked. The Conservative army executes him, as a deserter.

Jose Arcadio and Pilar Ternera have a son named Arcadio. Arcadio, a seemingly delicate child, grows up to become the town's schoolmaster. Regardless of the fact that Colonel Aureliano Buendia holds him accountable for Macondo's uprising, Arcadio demonstrates himself to be a despot who is fixated on hand. When traditionalists retake the town, he is executed. Arcadio is the father of Remedios the Beauty, Aureliano Segundo, and Jose Arcadio Segundo.

In the above mentioned characters, there exists the similarity in their preference of women. Both of them initially go after women much elder to them. While Aureliano Jose is obsessed with his aunt Amaranta, Arcadio unknowingly pursues his own biological mother, Pilar Ternera. In the case of Aureliano, it becomes his doom while Pilar Ternera's cleverness saves Arcadio from the unthinkable. Further, both these characters are executed by under the government forces for the paths they chose. Aureliano Jose was executed as a deserter from the rebel forces, where he joined as a means to escape the pangs of rejection from Amaranta. On the other hand, Arcadio who had turned himself into a tyrannical despot after being appointed by Colonel Aureliano as the administrator of Macondo, was executed by the government forces after the recapture of Macondo.Their doom was their own making.

Santa Sofa de la Piedad is a serene lady, almost imperceptible in this novel, who marries Arcadio and remains in the Buendia house for an extended period following his death, her aloofness watching out for the family. Remedios the Beauty, Aureliano Segundo, and Jose Arcadio Segundo are her children. In reality, she does not appear to exist, and when she becomes old and tired, she simply leaves the house, never to be seen or heard from again.

Fernanda del Carpio is Aureliano Segundo's wife and the mother of Meme, Jose Arcadio (III), and Amaranta Ursula. Fernanda del Carpio was raised by a group of devastated blue-bloods, and as a result, she is unusually haughty and strict. Her libertine husband does not adore her and continues to have an affair with Petra Cotes. In the meantime, Fernanda del Carpio makes futile attempts to impose her privileged lifestyle at the Buendia mansion.

It is intriguing to take note of fact that like the third era, even in the fourth era, the daughter-in-law of the family is similarly noisy in her methods of managing things. This ends up in the succeeding age to build up their own noisy conduct, some of which are like their archetypes. These characters are both aware of the wrong doings of their respective husbands. Yet, they never make serious attempts to correct them. They face cognitive dissonance in this aspect and their way of dealing with it was carry on with their household activities as it was their responsibility to keep the family in line. The responsibility of caring for the family being greater than correcting their husbands they both chose the former.

Jose Arcadio (III) is the eldest son of Aureliano Segundo and Fernanda del Carpio. In her assertion that Jose Arcadio (III) should be elected Pope, Ursula fails to realise that he is on the path to disintegration and isolation. Upon his return from his fruitless journey to theological school in Italy, Jose Arcadio (III) lives a life of depravity with a group of young people in the neighbourhood, who eventually murder him and steal his wealth from him. Jose Arcadio (III) realised during his life in theological college that there is no satisfaction in life lived on the terms of others. But, by then it was too late for him to do anything worthwhile, thus he makes his own way of life. He was bound to have faced cognitive dissonance in choosing to become a thief and turning young boys into thieves. He overcame the same in the prosperity that was offered by this path. Ultimately, he paid the price for his actions too.

Florentino Ariza, the main character of *Love in the Time of Cholera*, is a devoted and enthusiastic sex addict who is obsessed with the idea of love. Florentino falls head over heels in love with Fermina Daza right away. Having had a brief relationship during which he only saw Fermina in passing, he is unable to accept her rejection and vows to dedicate his life to one day winning her love back. He is looking forward to the death of Fermina's husband, Dr. Juvenal Urbino, who will have been married for fifty-one years, nine months, and four days when their troubled relationship comes to an end. Although he has an unending affection for Fermina, he sleeps with an infinite number of women; however, he is convinced that he is saving himself for her because he will never be able to cherish another lady in the same way that he has cherished Fermina. In the same way that an addict would use an opiate, Florentino uses sex to forget his sorrow and his desire for Fermina, the source of all his agony, as a means of escaping his misery.

Florentino Ariza is steadfast in his devotion to Fermina. But, he has no assurance that he would get her during his lifetime. Yet, he waited for the day he would get her. But, during the waiting period, he faces cognitive dissonance when he has to have physical relation with other women in order to exist, as he finds the physical pain of love unbearable. For him to sustain life, he had to relieve himself from the pain. Therefore, he accepted the temporary solution of maintaining sexual affairs with other women until the day he got the permanent solution which was the love of Fermina.

Throughout *Love in the Time of Cholera*, Fermina Dasa demonstrates herself to be a free, determined individual who is also refined and proficient. Dr.Urbino admires Fermina's steadfast, haughty levelheadedness and respects her for it. She is well aware of what she needs to do and will not rest until she has completed her task successfully. As a result of her husband's refusal to allow her to keep any of her non-speaking pet animals, she discovers one that can speak: a parrot. When she makes the decision to not excuse her husband until he admits his own fault, he promptly agrees to her terms. Taking responsibility for any wrongdoing is something she would never do; blame is the one emotion she cannot bear. Despite this, she appears to be a thoughtful, sustaining lady beneath her upbeat, steady exterior, as she treats her maturing husband like a vulnerable infant. Her obsessive fascination with animals and flowers is indicative of her ability to be resilient and caring.

Because of the numerous transitions Fermina must go through during her extended absence, it becomes clear that she has ended her relationship with Florentino without warning. She left the City of the Viceroys as a vulnerable young lady who has been cleansed by the fanatical longings of her first admirer, but she returns as a mature and complex young lady. As she grows into womanhood, she loses sight of the excitement of her forbidden feelings for Florentino, because it is no longer as outrageous or dangerous as it was when she was a child eager to defy her overbearing father. Eventually, she realises that her devotion to Florentino was nothing more than childish adoration of an unrealized fantasy, the realisation of a dream of a glorified man, and a romanticised sentiment. She feels compelled to continue forward into adulthood despite her realisation that she made a mistake in her earlier years of life.

In adulthood, she developed into a highly regarded individual deserving of admiration. By marrying Dr. Urbino, she ascends from the lower strata of the society to the pedigreed high class and maintains her position as a woman of society to the fullest extent possible. Her husband's plainly strict behaviour irritates her, as she is befuddled by Religion and the Church as a result of attending the Academy of the Presentation of the Blessed Virgin, an all-girls, Catholic school from which she is eventually expelled. Both, she believes, fall short of the uprightness preached to their followers. When the Doctor suggests, as he does on several occasions, that they include the Archbishop in their shaky marriage, she resolves, gladly declines, and perseveres, just as she does throughout the novel.

Fermina Dasa, as an individual, fought all her battles of life on her own. She lived life on her own terms. As a person dependant on her father and husband economically, she should surely face cognitive dissonance at varied phases of her life. She faces all the situations with the same mental strength which she used to continue her relationship with Florentino Ariza despite opposition from her father. While dealing with her husband she was at times clever while other times she was simply strict. In the case of her father, she dealt with him with her stubbornness.

In *The General in His Labyrinth*, Manuela Saenz is the General's long-term companion. She is also his first serious relationship since the death of his wife twenty- seven years earlier. Simon Bolivar's documented paramour Dona Manuela Saenz de Thorne, who Bolivar dubbed 'the liberator of the liberator' after she assisted him in escaping an assassination attempt on September 25, 1828, serves as the inspiration for her character. Because of Garcia Marquez's anecdotal portrayal of this verifiable figure, interest in her has re-ignited. She is increasingly being regarded, as Venezuelan historian Denzil Romero puts it, "perhaps the most important woman in Latin American History". (Jones) Her character is described as "the bold Quitena who loved him but was not going to follow him to his death" (*GHL* 6) in the novel.

Despite the fact that the General abandons Manuela Saenz, he continues to communicate with her throughout the novel. Additionally, she tries to write to him in order to provide him with information about the political situation; however, the mail carriers have been instructed not to acknowledge her letters. Manuela Saenz, like the historical Manuela Saenz, is married to Dr. James Thorne, an English physician more than twice her age, in the anecdotal Manuela Saenz's story. Manolo Saenz left Thorne after Bolivar wrote her a heartfelt letter in which he professed his undying love for her. A perceptive and unyielding character, she is described as having "irresistible grace, a sense of power, unbounded tenacity" (*GHL* 151) in the novel.

The actions of Manuela Saenz were always highly individualistic. Her decisions were often socially unacceptable or rather thought provoking. Her decision not to join the General in his final journey was well thought about. She was aware of her possible dangers in the absence of the General, but she chose not to witness the man she once loved ride into obscurity and his impending sad fate. Therefore, she did face cognitive dissonance, but overcame it with her decision to live with the mental image of the General with his greatness intact.

As the General's close companion, Field Marshal Antonio Jose de Sucre appears in the novel. In addition to being Simon Bolivar's closest confidant and right hand man, Antonio Jose de Sucre was also the Field Marshal of Ayacucho. Garcia Marquez portrays him as wise, methodical, timid, and eccentric, and he embodies these characteristics.

In addition to being married to Dona Mariana Carcelen, the Field Marshal is the father of a daughter with her. It is in the novel's central section that the General requests that Sucre take over as President of the Republic, but Sucre refuses to consider the request. As justification for his decision, Sucre provides a number of justifications, one of which is his desire to spend more time in the company of his family.

Field Marshall Sucre's choice of family over political position was indeed an individualistic choice. When he was offered the position of President, he refused it without any hesitation. As a man of integrity and courage, he knew that he would be able to discharge his duties to the people well. Yet, he chose not to accept the offer. He encountered cognitive dissonance in this choice but his desire to be available to his family overshadowed his desire to serve the people.

In *Of Love and Other Demons*, Father Cayetano Delaura, who is brought in for Sierva Maria's exorcism at first admits that she should not be exorcized. Delaura is attracted to romantic writing, including the affection verse of Garcilaso de la Vega, a Spanish writer to whom he guarantees inaccessible connection. His relationship with Sierva Maria fuels his battle between his common cravings and his Catholic obligations as a cleric, however eventually, heartfelt love surpasses him. Father Delaura despite being a priest vowed to celibacy becomes hopelessly enamoured with Sierva Maria and announces her, his adoration. Soon he starts visiting Sierva in her cell covertly, moving up from the sewer (that in future is fixed). They eat, rest, and discuss verse together. Later Father Cayetano is sent away to an outcast emergency clinic where he desires to get the infection however never does.

Delaura's affinity for romantic literature and affection for Sierva Maria are indicative of the emotional quandary that he is in. He knew that he had no training or skill to perform the exorcism nor did Sierva Maria need one. But, he is forced to accept the task upon insistence of the Bishop. He faced cognitive dissonance here and chose to spend time with Sierva Maria reading and reciting poems on the pretext of exorcism.

The focal character, Sierva Maria, a twelve-year-old young lady was born to a respectable family in decrease. Her folks, who never adored one another, disregard her from birth, so she is raised by the family's head slave, Dominga de Adviento. Truly, she is slim and pale with "taciturn blue" (*OLOD*, 12) eyes, and "pure copper" (*OLOD*, 12) hair that arrives at the ground and has been guaranteed to the holy people by Dominga. Growing up among the dark slaves, she receives their dialects, customs, and propensities, and has a serious doubt of white individuals. Sierva moves subtly with a practically powerful presence. She lies regularly and appears to appreciate making confusion. Father Delaura and Martina Laborde are the solitary two white individuals whom she comes to trust.

Sierva Maria's lifestyle was that she herself had invented. As she was raised by slaves she adopted certain of their traits alongside a few of her inherited traits. She seemed not to care for propriety or social customs. It would be hard to classify her behaviour as mere ignorance as she was an adolescent and not a child. She was able to overcome cognitive dissonance as she was aware of how and by whom she was raised. She seemed to feel that if she could be raised by people of African origin, she could certainly behave like one too.

Individualism in Love and Relationships

The kind of love affairs and relationships portrayed in *OneHundredYearsofSolitude* are highly individualistic. The major love affairs that blossom are those between Jose Arcadio and Pilar Ternera, Colonel Aureliano and Pilar Ternera, Rebecca and Pietro Crespi, Rebecca and Jose Arcadio (II), Amaranta and Gerinaldo, Aureliano Segnudo and Petra Cotes, Amaranta and Aureliano Jose, Meme and Mauricio Babilonia, and Amaranta Ursula and Aureliano. Almost all these relationships are, in the eyes of the society immoral. Some of them are also incestuous.

Relationships of Jose Arcadio and Colonel Aureliano with Pilar Ternera are mostly hidden from public view yet both bear fruit and they become the next generation of the Buendia family. These relationships invoke individualism as it was against social morality to solicit a prostitute. This situation becomes worse with Arcadio (son of Jose Arcadio and Pilar Ternera) as he, not knowing the truth, feels lustful of his mother. This situation is tactfully handled by Pilar Ternera.

Rebecca's relationships with Pietro Crespi and Jose Arcadio are problematic as well. Rebecca pursues Crespi only to spurn her stepsister Amaranta. While Crespi was initially inclined towards Amaranta, Rebecca snatches him from her. But, she does not marry him. Instead, she breaks up with him to marry her stepbrother. Though she is not related to Jose Arcadio by blood, this is indeed a problem from moralistic point of view. Her decision to break up with Crespi and her decision to marry Jose Arcadio are both individualistic and require a lot of courage to commit.

Amaranta on the other hand loses her ability to commit to love once she was discarded by Crespi and later his suicide. She raises Colonel Aureliano's son Aureliano like her own but the relationship turns shape very soon and Aureliano becomes obsessed with her. Initially, she does not oppose it, but later she understands the moral implications and breaks tie with Aureliano. In her later life, she shows interest in Colonel Gerinaldo but she does not let him pursue her more. Her guilty feelings turn her away from any kind of committed relationship. She therefore chose to remain single throughout her life.

Aureliano Segundo, the brother of Arcadio Segundo often exhibited all of the characteristics of his family's Jose Arcadios: he is enormous, disorderly, hasty, and epicurean in his eating habits. He is married to Fernanda del Carpio, with whom he has three children: Meme, Jose Arcadio (II), and Amaranta Ursula. His relationship with Petra Cotes is another hyper-individualistic love affair. On moral grounds, his relationships with his wife and his mistress are questionable, yet he makes room for both of them with a promise to his wife to die in her bed.

Meme and Mauricio Babilonia's relationship is the one that begins the ending of Buendia clan and Macondo. She goes against her mother's desire and continues her relationship with Babilonia. They are separated by her mother, who appoints guard to prevent Babilonia from seeing Meme. But, he secretly visits her at night, climbing into the house through the window, and is shot by the guard. It is later known that Meme had already bourne seed of the relationship, Aureliano. Meme is shipped off to a convent where she lives the remainder of her life. Considering the premarital status of the relationship, this relationship too was against social morality yet the couple was not ready to be stopped by anything.

The last among the list of individualistic relationship is the relationship between Aureliano and Amaranta Ursula. This incestuous relationship brought about the end of the Buendia clan.

The relationship between Aureliano and Amaranta Ursula blossoms after the wedding of the latter with Gaston. Gaston goes off to Europe on business and never returns when he gets to know about the affair of his wife. Despite them being related by blood, the relationship is allowed to continue. Amaranta Ursula gets pregnant as a result of the affair and dies in childbirth. The death of Amaranta Ursula drives Aureliano to alcoholism and ultimately losing his child, which is eaten by ants.

In *Love in the Time of Cholera,* Florentino Ariza's love for Fermina is similar to the disease cholera, which is accurate because he is in a real sense tormented by his feelings for her. He is insane with adoration, and he engages in over-the-top, borderline criminal behaviour. Fermina is followed by him, and he keeps an eye on her residence. He is completely depleted of all of his remaining energy for her, and he is unable to consider anything else. At work, he lacks the necessary skills to compose a business letter; instead, he can only compose idyllic compositions in the same manner as he does in his adoration letters to her. He blossoms as a result of his plague of adoration, and he takes pleasure in his own agony; he considers himself martyred when he is thrown in prison for entertaining Fermina with his fiddle. When Lorenzo Daza begins to take steps to shoot him, he challenges him, stating that it is generally considered honourable to be martyred in the name of adoration. Finally, he has made the decision to win Fermina's affectionate gestures, and he will work tirelessly to accomplish this goal. Instantaneously, he becomes the novel's antagonist and hero, depending on whether he is frantically in love or simply distraught.

Fermina, on her part, falls in love with Florentino at the persuasion of her aunt Escolastic. But, it is under her own decision that she continues her relationship. She is deeply committed in her affection to Florentino. It all happens at a very young age and, as she matures, she understands that all that existed between them was a mere illusion.

She immediately gives up the relationship, yet she stands her ground and opposes the advances of the doctor. Later, when the doctor pursues her and her father compels her to talk to him, she relents. But, it is the threatening anonymous letter that makes her accept the doctor's proposal. After the death of the doctor, Fermina is persuaded to rekindle the relationship with Florentino. What makes her decisions in these three instances are mainly the opposition that came from the social structures. In all these cases, she faced opposition from the external forces and that makes her go ahead with her decisions.

> "*Over the years they both reached the same wise conclusion by different paths: it was not possible to live together in any other way, or love in any other way, and nothing in this world was more difficult than love. (LTC223)*"

It had to be a mad dream, one that would give her the courage she would need to discard the prejudices of a class that had not always been hers but had become hers more than anyone's. It had to teach her to think of love as a state of grace: not the means to anything but the alpha and omega, an end in itself. (*LTC* 293)

In *TheGeneralinhisLabyrinth*, the relationship between the General and Manuela Saenz is a perfect example of individualism in love. They share a unique bond which cannot be defined within the confines of social norms. They keep their relationship a private affair though it is well known to the entire nation. Their relationship began by breaking the rules of the society, as Manuela broke out of her marriage for the same. They never had the intention of getting married and staying together but still they valued each other.

The General referred to her as the 'liberator of the liberator'. This is suggestive of her role in the General's life. "'You're a great man, General, greater than anyone,' she told him. 'But love is still too big for you.'" (*GHL*, 217) Finally, when the General sets off on his journey Manuela chooses to stay behind. Her decision could be seen as nothing but individualistic. "I'll never fall in love again... it's like having two souls at the same time." (*GHL*, 149) Therefore, the beginning and the end of the relationship were on the tones of individualism.

The relationships portrayed in *Of Love and Other Demons* are individualistic in its own terms. The major love relationships are those between Sierva and Father Delaura and Bernarda and Judas. Both these relationships could be seen as violation of social norms. In the case of Sierva and Delaura, it becomes immoral and individualistic as Delaura is a priest vowed to celibacy. As a priest, he is not supposed to have any relationship with a woman, but he goes against his moral obligation. He was there to exorcise Sierva but he was possessed by the girl and gave in to his desires. Furthermore, the age of Sierva is another issue of concern. She was a minor while Delaura was a much older man.

While for Sierva, no rules of the society or religion seemed to apply. She was mentally and emotionally free to do as she pleased and she chose to accept the bit of affection she got from Delaura. She had never received any affection from a man and when she had a chance, she accepted it readily. She read and recited poems with Delaura and found delight in what was offered.

Both of them got consolation and validation for the actions through the poems that they read together. "This was when she asked him whether it was true that love conquered all, as the songs said. 'It is true', he replied, 'but you would do well not to believe it'." (*OLOD*, 51)

> "*"For you was I born, for you do I have life, for you will I die, for you am I now dying." (OLOD, 94)*"

Conclusion

Individualism is the essence of every individual that sets him/ her apart from the rest. It is an individual's way of doing things, responding to situations and decision making. The fourth chapter of this thesis has taken this topic as its focal point. To a certain extent, individualism features as a personal trait in all the major characters of Garcia Marquez's works. This chapter deals with various aspects of individualism that are visible in these works.

The first aspect under consideration is individualism and society. Here characters and their actions are analysed from the perspective of behaviour and actions as opposed to societal expectations and norms. It is found that most characters face cognitive dissonance when they are forced to follow the norms of the society against their own desires. They generally overcome the dissonance and function as per their own desires. The second aspect is competitive individualism which spring as a result of competitive forces in the social environment. The characters are found to be in competition with their circumstances or others with the aim of fulfilling their desires. Again, cognitive dissonance which arises in their pursuit of goals is subdued innovatively.

The next aspect is methodological individualism, centres on the premise that incidents and phenomena cannot be explained without analysing the motivations and individual preferences. Methodological individualism is displayed by certain characters who invent their own ways to deal with their cognitive dissonance. The final aspect is that of individualism in love and relationship. The works of Garcia Marquez feature broad spectrum of love affairs. The individualism exhibited by characters when it comes to their love relationships is discussed in this section.

After a close examination of the cause and effect relationship of the individualism displayed by the characters and their results, it can be said that certain characters are successful in their venture while other end up failing or dying. Further, it is concluded that individualism is like a twin edged sword which can hurt the user and the opponent equally and should therefore be wielded carefully.

CHAPTER FOUR

HOPE AS A MOTIVATIONAL FACTOR

"Hope is the companion of power, and mother of success; for who so hopes strongly has within him the gift of miracles." - Smiles

Introduction

Hope can be described as a positive attitude in the mind which springs from an anticipation of good results in areas concerning life or the wider world. Dictionary definitions of the verb hope, "to cherish a desire with anticipation" and "expect with confidence". Despair, dejection, and hopelessness are some of the antonyms of hope.

Barbara Fredrickson, a renowned Psychology Professor, claims that hope springs at times of impending crisis, thereby leading one to new avenues of innovative ideas. She further claims that great necessities foster an even greater range of concepts and emotions both material and abstract like courage, strength, joy and happiness which originate from various areas within the self: physical, social, psychological, or cognitive perspectives.

People who harbour hope can be compared to "the little engine that could, [because] they keep telling themselves 'I think I can, I think I can'". (2002) When the basis of positive thinking is a realistic level of optimism rather than false hope, it leads to great results.

Richard Rorty (2000), a contemporary scholar, comprehends hope as something beyond objective setting, more like a metanarrative, a tale that fills in as a commitment or justification for anticipating a superior future. As a proponent of postmodernism, he accepts meta-fictions of the past, such as the Bible, utilitarianism, and Marxism were in fact false hopes; that hypothesis is unable to offer social expectation; and that liberal human beings should figure out how to live without a consensual hypothesis of social expectation. Rorty says another archive of commitment is required for social desire to exist once more. D. W. Winnicott (2012) viewed the acting out of a child as communicating an oblivious expectation to be cared for by the more extensive society, when regulation inside the close family had fizzled.

Object relations theory correspondingly sees the logical transaction as roused to some extent by an oblivious expectation that previous contentions and injuries can be managed once again. The Psychologist Charles R. Snyder connected hope to the presence of an objective, joined with a decided arrangement for arriving at that objective. Ernst Bloch and Alfred Adler had likewise contended for the centrality of hunting for objective in the psychology of humans. Snyder additionally focused on the connection among hope and mental self discipline, as well as the requirement for a sensible view of objectives, contending that the distinction among positive mindset and hopefulness was that the latter included useful pathways to a better future.

Among the infinite patterns that look at the significance of hope in a person's life, there are two significant speculations that have acquired a lot of acknowledgment in the discipline of psychology. One of these speculations, created by Charles R. Snyder, contends that hope ought to be seen as a mental expertise that exhibits a person's capacity to keep up the drive while chasing a specific objective. This model reasons that a person's capacity to be confident relies upon two sorts of reasoning: agency thinking and pathway thinking.

Agency thinking alludes to a singular's assurance to accomplish their objectives notwithstanding potential obstructions, while pathway thinking alludes to the manners by which a person accepts they can accomplish these individual objectives.

Hope Theory

Snyder's hypothesis involves hope as a component that is most frequently found in psychotherapy. In these occurrences, the practitioner assists their patient with defeating boundaries that have kept them from accomplishing objectives. The practitioner would then assist the client with putting forth sensible and pertinent individual objectives, that is, "I am going to find something I am passionate about and that makes me feel good about myself" (2010), and help the patient in retaining their confidence in their skills and possibility of accomplishing their aims and objective.

Snyder's theory centres on hope as an instrument for a person to conquer absence of inspiration to accomplish objectives, whereas Kaye A. Herth theory manages a person's future objectives as they connect with adapting to diseases. Herth perceives hope as "a motivational and cognitive attribute that is theoretically necessary to initiate and sustain action toward goal attainment".(Arnau et al., 2010) Laying out practical and feasible objectives in this present circumstance is more troublesome, as the person undoubtedly does not have direct command over the fate of their wellbeing. Rather, Herth recommends that the objectives ought to be focused on how the person will actually manage the disease - "Instead of drinking to ease the pain of my illness, I am going to surround myself with friends and family" (ibid). Though the idea of the objectives in Snyder's model varies with those in Herth's model, the two of them perceive hope as a method for keeping up with individual inspiration, which eventually will bring about a more prominent feeling of good faith.

Hope, and all the more explicitly, specific hope, has been demonstrated to be a significant piece of the recuperation cycle from sickness; it has solid mental advantages for patients, assisting them with adapting all the more to their illness. For instance, hope propels individuals to seek after solid ways of behaving for recuperation, like eating fresh foods and natural food, stopping smoking, and making a workout routine. In addition to upgrading individuals' recuperation from sicknesses, these practices prevent further or new illnesses. Patients who keep up with elevated degrees of hope have a better visualisation for hazardous ailment and an improved personal satisfaction. Conviction and assumption, which are key components of hope, block torment in patients experiencing persistent ailment by delivering endorphins and imitating the impacts of morphine. Subsequently, through this cycle, conviction and assumption can set off a chain response in the body that can make recuperation from constant disease more probable. This chain response is particularly clear with studies exhibiting the placebo effect, a circumstance when hope is the main variable supporting these patients' recuperation.

Generally, studies have shown that keeping a feeling of hope during a time of recuperation from disease is valuable. A feeling of sadness during the recuperation time frame has, on many occasions, brought about unfavourable medical issues for the patient (for example sadness and nervousness following the recuperation interaction). Furthermore, having a more noteworthy measure of trust previously and during mental treatment has prompted diminished Post-Traumatic Stress Disorder related misery side effects in war veterans. Hope has additionally been viewed as related with additional positive impressions of abstract wellbeing. Nonetheless, surveys of examination writing have noticed that the associations among hope and seriousness of symptoms in other psychological wellness issues are less clear, like in instances of people with schizophrenia.

The consideration of hope in healing methods could a have crucial impact in fields of both psychological and physical wellness. Hope as a component for further developed therapy has been concentrated on with regards to Post-Traumatic Stress Disorder, persistent physical diseases, and fatal illnesses, among different issues and infirmities. Inside psychological health studies, practitioners have proposed involving trust mediations as an enhancement to additional rudimentary mental and behavioural treatments. As far as help for physical sickness, research proposes that hope can support the arrival of endorphins and enkephalins, which help to avoid torment.

There are two fundamental contentions in view of judgement against the people who are promoters of utilising hope to assist with treating extreme ailments. Among these the first is assuming doctors have an excessive amount of hope, they may forcefully treat the patient. The doctor will clutch a little sliver of hope that the patient might improve.

Hence, this makes them attempt techniques that are exorbitant and may make many extra complications. One doctor reported that she lamented having hope for her patient; it brought about her patient enduring three additional years of torment that the patient could not have possibly persevered assuming the doctor had acknowledged recuperation was impossible.

The subsequent contention is the division among hope and wishing. Those that are confident are effectively attempting to examine the best way of move while making into thought the deterrents. Research has shown however that a large number of the people who have hope are unrealistically thinking and latently making a half-hearted effort, as though they are trying to feign ignorance about their genuine conditions. Being trying to claim ignorance and having an excess of hope may adversely affect both the patient and the doctor.

The effect that hope can have on a patient's recuperation interaction is unequivocally upheld through both observational exploration and hypothetical methodologies.

Notwithstanding, surveys of writing likewise keep up with that more longitudinal and strategically sound examination is expected to lay out which hope mediations are really the best, and in what setting (for example constant disease versus terminal ailment).

In the question of globalisation, hope is centred around monetary and social strengthening. Coming to certain Asian countries, trust has taken on a mainstream or materialistic structure corresponding to the quest for financial development. Essential models are the ascent of the economies of China and India, relating with the idea of Chindia. An optional important model is the expanded utilisation of contemporary design in rising economies, for example, the construction of the Shanghai World Financial Centre, Burj Khalifa and Taipei 101, which has led to an overarching hope inside the nations of beginning.

In turbulent conditions, hope is risen above without social limitations, exiled Syrian children are upheld by UNESCO's schooling project through imaginative training and psycho-social help. More help for imparting hope beyond cultural barriers includes food culture, separating evacuees from injury through drenching them in their rich social past.

Hope in Literature

Hope can be utilised as an imaginative plot gadget and is much of the time a rousing power for change in unique characters. A normally perceived reference from western mainstream society is the caption "A New Hope" from Episode IV in the Star Wars sci-fi space show. The caption alludes to one of the lead characters, Luke Skywalker, who is supposed in the future to permit great to win over abhorrent inside the plot of the movies.

The swallow has been an image of hope, in Aesop's tales and various other memorable literary works. It represents hope, to some extent since it is among the principal birds to show up toward the close of winter and the beginning of spring. Some other images of hope incorporate the anchor and the pigeon.

Elpis (Hope) shows up in old Greek folklore with the account of Zeus and Prometheus. Prometheus took fire from the God, Zeus, which maddened the preeminent god. Thus, Zeus made a crate that contained all habits of insidiousness, unbeknownst to the collector of the case. Pandora opened the crate in the wake of being cautioned not to, and released a large number of hurtful spirits that caused maladies, sicknesses, and diseases on humankind. Spirits of insatiability, envy, scorn, doubt, distress, outrage, vengeance, desire, and sadness dispersed all over searching for people to torture. Inside the crate, be that as it may, there was likewise an unreleased mending soul named Hope. From old times, individuals have perceived that a feeling of hope had the ability to recuperate burdens and assists them with bearing seasons of extraordinary misery, sicknesses, fiascos, misfortune, and torment brought about by the vindictive spirits and occasions. In Hesiod's Works and Days, the representation of hope is named Elpis.

Norse folklore anyway thought about Hope (Von) to be the drool dribbling from the mouth of Fenris Wolf. Their idea of fortitude evaluated most profoundly a happy grit without a trace of hope. Hope is a vital idea in most significant world religions, frequently meaning the 'hoper' accepts that an individual or an aggregate gathering will arrive at an idea of paradise. Contingent upon the religion, hope should be visible as an essential for as well as by result of profound fulfilment.

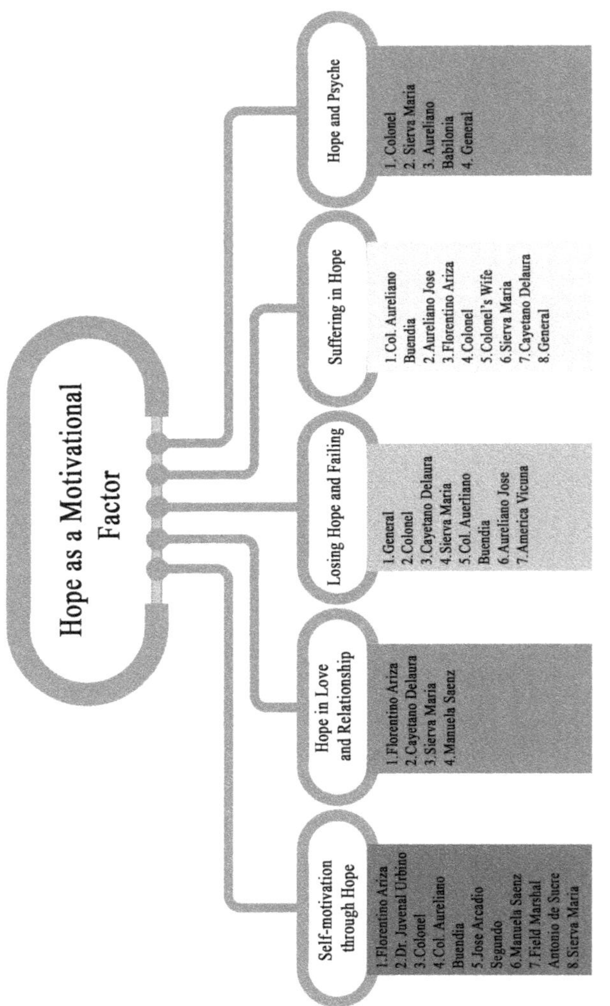

Chart 5.1

Characters Harbouring Hope

Self-motivation through Hope

In *Love in the Time of Cholera*, Florentino Ariza displays high self-motivation which is derived through hope of attaining his goal. When it comes to his wait for Fermina Dasa, he genuinely hopes that someday she would accept his love. He waits for her for more than fifty years. But, he was determined to prove himself worthy of her.

He understood the difference in their respective social statuses and made sure that he would somehow reach up-to that level. He consistently works his way up and becomes the President of the river boat company by the time Fermina's husband dies. It was with that confidence that he declared his undying love for her at the vigil for the doctor. Furthermore, in his pursuit of women to ease his pain of being separated from Fermina, he faces rejection on many occasions. Yet, he was persistent in his effort and ultimately won over all of them.

Dr. Juvenal Urbino, the husband of Fermina Dasa, is another character who displays self-motivation. He was deeply affected by the death of his father, who was also a doctor, due to cholera. He made it his mission in life to fight against the epidemic. When the city administration was at a loss, he took up the responsibility and almost single-handedly saved the city. It was his vision that improved the sanitation facilities in the working class neighbourhoods of the city. He was motivated by the trauma in his personal life and took to it with the hope of saving lives. Even in the case of his marriage to Fermina, he was persistent despite her initial rejection. Fermina was repulsed by him due to the circumstances of their first meeting. It forbade her from accepting his advances but he pursued her more vigorously. Though it was his social status that made Lorenzo Dasa to persuade his daughter to accept his courtship, at long last Urbino succeeded in wooing her.

No One Writes to the Colonel moves forward with the theme of positive hope. The protagonist, the Colonel, determined solidarity to beat every one of his challenges in life through hope. The difficulties of the Colonel never truly finished with the completion of the novella. His concerns persevered yet he was as yet hopeful.

It is this soul of energy that assists any individual with prevailing throughout everyday life. The Colonel gripped on to his two significant expectations. The first was the appearance of his benefits checks and the second, of his chicken entering a battle and getting cash. Hopefulness alone cannot lead an individual to progress. Alongside hope, the individual needs to continue to work toward the path. Here, the Colonel was confident of his chicken, and he likewise gave great consideration to it regardless of his neediness. He even dropped the arrangement with Colonel Sabas and brought back the chicken. He did everything humanly conceivable to satisfy his expectation. In the event of the annuity checks, all he could do was to consistently check with the mailing station.

He was persistent in that too. It must be noted that his hope was not backed by anyone else. He propelled himself forward each day and fought the odds. This is a standing testament to his anticipated victory in the days to come and turns him into a legitimate hero. Further, the open-ended closing of the novella leaves room for the reader to hope for a positive ending to the Colonel's story.

Colonel Aureliano in *One Hundred Years of Solitude* is another character who appears to be highly self-motivated and moves forward with hope. Nothing and no person ever touched him emotionally. Remedios Moscote, his underage wife appears to be the only emotional bond that happens to him. Yet, after her passing, he understands that the distress is not as significant as he had anticipated. During the conflict, he turns out to be significantly more solidified to feeling, and, at last, his memory and every one of his sentiments are eroded. Toward the finish of his life, he has quit making new brilliant fish. All things considered, he makes twenty five of them and afterward dissolves them down, utilising the metal for the following cluster. Along these lines, he lives exclusively in the present, recognizing cyclical nature of time and that the present is all that exists for a man like him, without any recollections.

Jose Arcadio Segundo, the grand nephew of Colonel Aureliano Buendia, dismayed by seeing an execution at an early age, grew-up to be meagre, hard, singular and progressively insightful, similar to his incredible uncle, the colonel. A chicken warrior and a wanderer, he found reason in driving the strikers against the banana organisation. He was the last one standing of the slaughter of the strikers. His endeavours to remind individuals about the slaughter go to no end as nobody trusts him. Getting strength from the inside, he goes to incredible stretches out to take the slaughter back to the personalities of individuals. At the point when he finds that no one accepts the slaughter happened, he separates himself in Melquiades‘ old review, attempting to translate the old predictions and safeguarding the memory of the slaughter.

Manuela Saenz from *The General in His Labyrinth* is highly self-motivated and goes on in life with positivity. She had been previously married to an English doctor but she left the confines of married life to join the General in an openly secretive relationship. The General referred to her as the liberator of the liberator, this shows her significance in his life. She is more like a mother-figure to him, as she sheltered him as his paramour and as a companion for eight years after the death of his wife. The fact that she would not "follow him to his death" (*GHL*, 6) shows how morally strong she is. She knew that he had lost his hope and was journeying towards his doom. It was unbearable to her that he had ceased to become anything but a shadow of the man he was. Instead of watching him sink further, she chose to maintain within her mind the image of the man he was. Thus, she becomes the tragic yet headstrong heroine of the novel.

Field Marshal Antonio de Sucre is another character from *The General in His Labyrinth* who is highly self-motivated. He had reached the rank of Field Marshal and thus had the possibility of succeeding the General as the President of Gran Colombia. He was also asked by the General to do so, but he chose not to. Instead, he wanted to lead a normal life with his family. Here, the Field Marshal's self-motivation is quite evident as he gave up an opportunity to become the President in favour of living for his own family.

Sierva Maria from *OfLoveandOtherDemons,*in her behaviour and beliefs, appears to be deeply self-motivated. Her linguistic ability is a prominent feature that shows her self-motivation. Being raised by the household slaves, she spoke African dialects from a young age which was quite normal. But, as a child she was bound to have identified her true lineage and switch to her mother-tongue. She never did that. She continued to use foreign tongues which would be seen as an abomination. Yet, she was not bothered by the public gaze. The same could be said about her choice in clothes and ornaments. She wears stone necklaces like the slaves do. Here too, her social status and social expectation does not bother her. She determined the course of her life till the end. Her ability to escape from the straight jacket and shackles and deliver a debilitating kick to the Bishop's lower abdomen during the exorcism is proof of her desire to live. This incident gained prominence due to the fact that she had been starving herself for a week leading up to this. Finally, she gives up her struggle when she loses her only hope as Cayetano had been sent away.

Hope in Love and Relationship

Love in the Time of Cholera depicts the highest level of hope in love. The central characters, Florentino Ariza and Fermina Dasa, fall in love with each other at a young age. It goes on for a short period before her father discovers it and sends her away to live with relatives. Even when they were separated, they corresponded in regular intervals.

But, when she returns to the city and meets Florentino Ariza, she comes to the conclusion that all that existed between them was a mere illusion. She further distances herself from Florentino Ariza. Florentino Ariza, on his part, is unable to forget her or be separated from her. Soon, Fermina Dasa gets married to a renowned physician in the town.

Florentino Ariza realises that at his current situation he would not be able to match up to Dr. Urbino in his social status. He understands that he would have to wait for the death of Dr. Urbino to get a chance to woo Fermina Dasa again. Meanwhile, he decides to make himself worthy of her by climbing the social ladder of wealth and status. He does this by joining the river boat company as a clerk. As thirty years pass, he becomes the President of the company and gains respect in the society. Now, all he needed was for Dr. Urbino to pass, so that he could pursue Fermina Dasa again. Years pass by and the day he waited for arrived – more than fifty years after he was rejected by Fermina Dasa.

He takes his chance and is immediately turned down by Fermina Dasa, who throws him out of the house during the vigil of her husband. He does not give up even then. He writes her a long letter on the reflection of life and it makes her reconsider. They get back in touch over frequent evening tea and ultimately rekindle their relationship. Here, it must be noted that Florentino Ariza was hopeful of somehow winning over Fermina Dasa. He never gave up on his goal. He kept on working on his shortcomings and achieved his objective.

The relationship between Father Cayetano Delaura and Sierva Maria in *OfLoveand OtherDemons*is one that has a twisted sense of hope hidden deep inside. This relationship is wrong in two folds. The first, being the age of Sierva. She was merely twelve years old while Father Delaura was thrice that much. The second reason is his status as a priest vowed to celibacy. These reasons prevent any one of sane mind to think of the relationship as anything beyond a statutory rape. It appears that hope was the key element that fuelled the relationship between Sierva Maria and Delaura.

While considering Sierva Maria, it could be said that she met Delaura in the abyss of her despair and discovered rejuvenated hope in his soothing words and affectionate behaviour. The time she spent with Delaura reading and reciting love poetry was her only solace at a time of extreme solitude and torment. It was this hope that gave the strength to endure the torture and isolation in the name of exorcism. This hope kept her alive despite all odds. Once it was lost, she was unable to continue and she died.

Delaura's hope on the other hand was focused on the fact that his relationship with Sierva Maria would not come out in the public and cause him any harm. Since Sierva Maria was already isolated from the society and demonised in the community, there was no way the relationship would be detected. Even if Sierva Maria spoke about it to anyone, it would only be considered as the rambling of an insane girl possessed by evil spirits. Therefore, he went on with the relationship. But, as time progressed, his hope was overcome by guilt towards his divine duty and he confessed to the Bishop.

The General in His Labyrinth is a meta-narration of the final seven months of Simon de Bolivar, saviour and President of Gran Colombia by Garcia Marquez. The book follows Bolivar's last process from Bogota to the Caribbean shore of Colombia in his endeavour to leave South America for exile in Europe. Doing away with the conventional chivalrous depiction of Bolivar El Libertador, Garcia Marquez portrays a lamentable hero, a rashly matured man who is genuinely sick and intellectually depleted. The story investigates the maze of Bolivar's life through the account of his recollections, wherein gloom, ailment, and passing unavoidably prevail upon affection, wellbeing, and life.

Manuela Saenz moved forward in her relationship with the General high in hope. When the General seemed to have lost all hope in life and decided to relinquish his title as the President and move to Europe, she decided against going with him in his decrepit state. It was a bold move on her part to do this as they were each other's sole companions.

Her decision not follow the General to his death appears to have two implications. The first is that it could serve as motivating factor for the General to come back to her. She sincerely hoped that he would return to the capital as his former self. The second is that she was unable to watch the General sink deep in despair and rather she would live on the image of the General with all his vitality and vigorous nature. She could not let that image fade away under any circumstance. Therefore, she hung on to her hope and wished for the General to find his hope and return.

Hopelessness and Failure

The novel *The General in His Labyrinth* begins as the General was setting off on his exile to the port city of Cartagena de Indias, from where he had needed to go to Europe. He had recently surrendered his title as the President of Gran Colombia. Lamentably, he sees that residents of the country he liberated have now sold out him, scribbling on the walls against Bolivar, splash painting and throwing waste at him. This was the primary catastrophe for his confidence and hope. The General's lack of distinction is portrayed vividly in all sections of the book. He is truly stunned at the new turn of events and his will cripples with every second that passes. His disintegrating physical, which makes him unrecognisable, can be credited to his shortfall of will and trust.

As the convoy progresses, his genuine shortcoming and pride are clear as he orchestrates the inclination to the dock: he should have been conveyed anyway he would not yield to it. The General's team remains a night in Puerto Real, where the General seems to fantasize. He pronounces to have seen a woman anyway his confidants could not find her after an elaborate search. In the next city on his way, people really trust him to be the President of Gran Colombia and prepare meals in his honour; but these festivals are wasted on him as a result of his shortfall of fortitude and hankering. His actual state decays reliably, making a visitor depict his face as a dead man's face. General Daniel Florencio O'Leary goes with new understanding about persistent political new developments. Joaquin Mosquera, named as his substitute as President of Gran Colombia, has acknowledged power yet his realness is at this point tested by General Rafael Urdaneta. Hearing this, the General says that his "dream began to fall apart on the very day it was realized" (*GHL*, 153).

The General at long last gets his documents and passport, and before long he sets off with his escort for Cartagena and the coast. In Cartagena, different parties are held in his honour. In any case he is surrounded by ladies, during this time, it ends up being clear to the peruser that his virility is lost. The last disaster for his will is the ambush and murder of his friend and comrade in arms,

Field Marshal Sucre. The General is before long told by one of his companions that General Rafael Urdaneta has assumed control of the public master in Bogota, and there are reports of shows and upheavals on a re-appearance of force by Bolivar.

The General's escort goes to the town of Soledad, where he remains for over a month, his flourishing declining further. In Soledad, the General consents to see an expert unusually. It is puzzling whether to recognize this as the disintegrating of his supposition or his reclamation. The General never leaves South America. He finishes his journey in Santa Marta, excessively weak to try and contemplate continuing and with simply his confidants and his closest colleagues nearby. He passes on in poverty, a miserable leftover of the person who liberated a huge area of the continent.

Bolivar is portrayed as a miserable leftover of the man he was. He has lost all the centrality in his life. He was viewed as a superhuman by people in his country, but in the final days portrayed in the book. He is a fragile man trapped in the maze of his own mind. He trusts very much to be returned to by the occupants. Be that as it may, he makes no step towards fulfilling his assumption. Rather, he absorbs despair when he finds that the very people he gave liberality have sold out him. The last calamity for him is the destruction of all his accepted accomplices by the gathering of his strategic opponents whom he had held back from procuring control up to that point.

A major theme of *NoOneWritestoColonel*is hope and the lack thereof. The central character, The Colonel has endlessly hoped for over half a century for something better to come along, including the arrival of his pension and the payoff from having the rooster in his possession. It is this hope that keeps him sustained, till the end of the novel, the colonel never deserts his hope. The protagonist, the Colonel has waited hopefully over fifty years for a positive turn of events, including the appearance of his annuity and the result from fighting a rooster he owned. This hope keeps him going, till the close of the novel. The colonel never deserts his expectation. In any event, when he has no clue about what he and his spouse will eat while they trust that the chicken will pay off, he never forsakes trust and that is authoritative evidence that he would make due and succeed.

No One Writes to the Colonel recapitulates the story of an unnamed veteran in his late-70s, who was a colonel in the Thousand Days' War, a Colombian nationwide conflict at the turn of the millennium. The matured colonel and his spouse live in a destroyed town, stricken by oppressive political viciousness and savage bureaucrats and wealthy individuals. Disregarding the way that the colonel played a crucial role in the Thousand Days' War a very long time earlier, conveying "the funds for the civil war in two trunks roped to the back of a mule" (*NWC*, 26), the Colonel has never gotten his retirement benefits.

No matter what the miserable situation, each Friday the colonel walks around the mail station at the harbour and waits for the arrival of the mail. The postmaster has a negative outlook towards the colonel's merriment, unveiling to him that, "no one writes to the colonel" (*NWC*, 21). The colonel's wife, too, comprehends the annuity would never come and following a long time of bafflement and close starvation, uncovers to her better half that they cannot "eat hope" (*NWC*, 39).

Hence, one might say that the presence and lack of hope is the distinction among life and demise. In *No One Writes to the Colonel*, the Colonel is highly confident in his life and despite everything expects a superior future. He never leaves it to his destiny neither does he quit hoping in the apparently impossible cheerful closure of his life.

He has experienced a wide range of torments throughout everyday life. He needed to confront the disappointment of the insubordination and give up despite his desire to the contrary, he confronted destitution with elegance, he likewise lost his child, yet he stood unfaltering to his convictions. This battle made him more grounded continuously and thus reinforced his expectation. In this manner, he lives on.

The novella opens with the death of a *youth*, “the first death from natural causes” (*NWC*, 6) the town has had for "many years" (*NWC*, 6). The Colonel’s son, Augustin, was killed by the military for “distributing clandestine literature” (*NWC*, 11). From Augustin, the Colonel obtained a chicken, used in cockfighting. The chicken holds a likelihood of securing cash if it fights well, yet the old couple cannot bear bolstering the chicken and themselves. The colonel’s significant other considers the chicken a “expensive illusion” (*NWC*, 11) but the colonel harbours hope in its payoff, just as much as his hope in his pension.

Disregarding the way that the colonel and his soulmate live on the shaky edge of starvation, without any assumption for compensation, the colonel’s honour and pride stay perfect. He won’t allow his significant other an opportunity to sell their two or three resources; in the event that anyone finds they were starving. At his wife’s solicitation, the colonel offers the chicken to his comrade, Sabas, a fellow veteran who ended up rich through spearheading political commitments. The colonel, regardless, reneges on the game plan and recuperates the chicken. At the novella’s end, the colonel’s life partner asks the colonel in restlessness what they will eat. The colonel answers that they will eat "shit" (*NWC*, 62).

Hope and its power appear to be a major theme in *Of Love and Other Demons*. Sierva Maria endures a great deal of torture both at the hands of the Bishop when she is incarcerated for her alleged demonic possession and the society which demonises and isolates her for her ‘differentness’. Throughout her life, she was targeted for her strange behaviour which according to the society and the church was not normal. Her illness, which was the result of a dog-bite, was termed as demonic possession. She was thrown in a cell and forced to undergo torturous exorcism techniques. But, all this while, she held up her beliefs and went on her own way. It was possible for her only due to her hope in life.

The love between her and Delaura was the source of her hope. When Delaura is unable to bear his guilt of betraying his faith, he confesses to the Bishop, who took measures to separate the lovers. This resulted in Sierva Maria losing hope. She was thus unable to go ahead and bear the punishment of exorcism. Moreover, the fate of Delaura hurt her even more, as he was put to public trial and humiliation. It was then that she turned violent during her exorcism sessions and finally died of “love”, when she had in fact died of hopelessness.

Delaura on the other hand had an even worse fate due to hopelessness. His hope of never getting caught let him engage in the relationship with Sierva Maria. But, his guilt overcame his hope and ultimately made him confess. When he is sent off to care for lepers at the outcaste hospital, he finds false hope of salvation through suffering. While caring for lepers, he hopes to get the disease and die. This is indicative of his hopelessness. His guilt has thus led him down the path of destruction and hopelessness.

The characters of Colonel Buendia and Aureliano (II) in *One Hundred Years of Solitude* exhibit hopelessness. For Colonel Buendia, it was the surrender of his compatriots that caused hopelessness. He was quite confident that the rebellion would bear fruit but when the government offers truce, his comrades are tempted to accept it and lay down their arms. Colonel Buendia is thus forced to accept the peace offering and surrender as it was futile to continue the war alone. Though he does not accept defeat, his failure is visible in his lifestyle. His withdrawal from public life and retreating to his goldfish making is symbolic of his failure.

Even after the failure of the rebellion Colonel Buendia harboured a vague hope which he accidentally spilled out in an outburst of frustration at the oppressive activities of the conservative government. He expressed his desire to arm his seventeen sons and restart the rebellion. Although he had no real intention to reorganise the rebellion and this statement was a mere emotional outburst, it led to his final defeat and loss of hope. His statement was taken by the conservative government as a serious threat and they arranged for a systematic extermination of the Colonel’s legacy. Ultimately, all but one of his sons are killed and the remainder goes into hiding until his final day when he is shot dead at the doorsteps of the Buendia house.

Aureliano (II) was forced into a reclusive life by his grandmother owing to his illegitimate birth. He formed a deep and incestuous relationship with his maternal aunt Amaranta Ursula. The relationship caused the breakage of Amaranta Ursula's marriage. Aureliano (II) emerges into the society after the death of his grandmother. He found it hard to cope with the society as it was quite unfamiliar to him. His relationship with Amaranta Ursula bore fruit and it was a child with a pigtail as the prophecy had suggested. But, his loss of hope springs from the death of Amarata Ursula. She was his sole companion in the world from his birth. She was his connection to the world. Her loss was unbearable to him and led him to alcoholism which caused further problems as he misplaced his son while he was intoxicated. The child ended up getting eaten by ants and thus he loses his purpose and hope in life. This loss of hope is the reason for his calm acceptance of fate after he deciphered the prophecy of Melquiades.

America Vicuna in *Love in the Time of Cholera* is a character who loses hope and ends up failing in life. She had been in a secret relationship with Florentino Ariza. They were able to keep their relationship under the radar of the society due to their difference in age and Florentino's status as her local guardian. For Florentino, she was just one of his many trysts to escape from his pangs of being separated from Fermina. But, for Vicuna, he was her first experience in love. He had introduced her to a new of world physical pleasure and excitement. When he announced his decision to get married, she was heartbroken and lost all interest in school. Her loss of hope causes her to ignore studies and consequently fail in exams. She then commits suicide as she had lost her purpose in life. Therefore, loss of hope in life was undoubtedly the reason for her suicide.

Suffering in Hope

Colonel Aureliano in *One Hundred Years of Solitude* is a character who suffered all through his life while harbouring hope even in the face of defeat. He is the true embodiment of solitude portrayed in the novel. He is constantly surrounded by people while being isolated from them all. Remedios Moscote, his child wife, is the only person who has a profound influence on him. But, that too, ends with her tragic death. Thereafter, his sole existence is for the revolution. After many years of fighting, the rebellion fails and the rebels surrender to the government forces.

Colonel Aureliano's spirit was not defeated even then. Yet, he is compelled to give up arms after all the other rebel leaders agree to the treaty and withdraw their troops. Before his surrender, once when he was captured and faced the firing squad, his hope did not waver. But, later when he finds his existence pointless, he is tired of his suffering and puts a bullet to his heart, which again misses its mark and fails to end his misery. He is thus forced to live out his miserable life, finding solace in his golden fishes.

Aureliano Jose, the Colonel's son with Pilar Ternera is another character who suffers in hope in *One Hundred Years of Solitude*. As a child away from his mother, he was raised by his aunt, Amaranta. Amaranta, in her turn, was an unmarried woman and showered her affections on him, which caused an unhealthy obsession towards her in the mind of Aureliano. As he grew up, this obsession grew up with him while Amaranta deliberately tried to keep a healthy distance from him. But, Aureliano was unable to think of any other and stayed fixated on her.

Dejected by her indifference towards him, he follows in his father's footsteps and joins the rebel forces. This could be seen as a desperate step from his side to forget the pain of rejection. But, he is unable to stay in the rebel army and deserts his post. He goes back to Amaranta in hopes of being accepted into her life. Once again he is rejected and he goes back to his post, but he is intercepted by the government forces on the way and is summarily executed. His life ended as a result of his suffering which was based on hope.

Love in the Time of Cholera is a novel, which unwinds a universe of force, both imperialistic and male centric. Yet, it is likewise a novel about adoration. At one level it is a straightforward circle of drama story wherein two men and one lady play the lead roles. In any case, a top to bottom investigation of the connections uncovers that in adoration and marriage, the lady is the victim on the grounds that both love and marriage are constrained by man and he does not permit a lady to go past his directions and the standards set somewhere near him. Preceding marriage, a lady's life is constrained by her dad, after marriage by her spouse and it is solely after the demise of the spouse that she might have the option to practise her will and express her cravings and that as well, on the off chance that she is sufficiently able to oppose the general public around her. Fermina Daza, the protagonist of the novel is one such lady who experiences because of her dad and her significant other yet subsequent to encountering a lot of aggravation and enduring she leaves the familial snare.

Florentino Ariza suffers a great deal in hope of reattaining the affection of his beloved. After the initial breakup with Florentino, Fermina gets married to Dr. Urbino and Florentino vows that he would stay loyal to Fermina until the death of Dr. Urbino to win her back while trying to make himself worthy of her. He patiently waits for the day of Dr. Urbino's death. It takes more than half a century for Dr. Urbino to finally die.

Florentino grew to be the President of the river boat company by this time. But, it was not quite easy for him to while away fifty years. He suffers both physical and mental pain due to his separation from Fermina. His longing for her had several implications to his physical and mental health. He suffered choleric symptoms and nausea as a direct result of his attempts to capture her essence and scent by eating flowers and drinking cologne. When his mother sees his torment, she suspects it to be cholera. But, later, when she understands that it was the pain of love, she is relieved and tells him to enjoy it as it would not last for long. Her advice was to derive pleasure from the pain which he was unable to do as the pain itself was unbearable to him. He moved forward in his life, always carrying this pain and being obsessed with Fermina. But, after being forced upon by a mysterious woman in the river boat, he had discovered the 'painkiller' to his condition.

In *No One Writes to the Colonel*, the Colonel and his wife suffer a great deal in hope. The Colonel, being the optimist that he is, stays quite confident that he would surely get the pension cheques that were promised to him. He and his wife live a life of poverty and illness related to old age. This suffering was indeed the result of the hope of the pension cheques. He was ready to starve himself but would not give up his hope. Furthermore, the rooster left to him by his son Augustin is another factor that supplies hope to the Colonel. He along with the whole town believed that the rooster would win a lot of fights and bring wealth to them.

Considering the positivity in his mind, the Colonel's suffering is acceptable while that of his wife is not as her sufferings were not caused by her own hope but that of her husband's hope. Since the Colonel believes that his hope's desires would surely come true he is able to bear the sufferings without complaint. But, his wife does not share his belief and therefore does not have the mental strength to overcome the pains. Her only hope lies in the positivity of her husband. Yet, that is not sufficient to endure the suffering, hence she is often found lamenting and complaining.

In *Of Love and Other Demons*, Sierva Maria and Delaura endure pain and suffering in their hope. While Sierva Maria suffers in the hope of being accepted and recognised as what she was, Delaura suffers in the hope of salvation. The suffering of both Sierva Maria and Delaura are inflicted by the Bishop. Sierva Maria underwent suffering in the form of exorcism and isolation due to her behaviour which according to the Bishop was out of the way. She endures the pain not knowing how to comply or what constitutes 'normal' behaviour. Her hope was to be understood and accepted for her true identity. In the meantime, she also found hope in the form of love from Delaura. This hope gives her the strength to bear the torturous exorcism techniques. But, with the exile of Delaura, she lost that hope and drew her last breath.

Delaura's suffering was partly self-afflicted as he confessed about his 'sinful' relationship with Sierva Maria to the Bishop which resulted in his exile. He felt guilty in his undertaking as he was a priest vowed to celibacy. He found hope in his punishment to serve at the outcaste hospital. He hoped to redeem his soul through service to lepers. Furthermore, he desired to get the disease and die. His hope of salvation was in death and redemption, which cannot be considered a positive attitude but to him it was apparently the righteous path.

In *The General in His Labyrinth*, the General too afflicts sufferings upon himself. He suffered a great deal during journey down the Magdalena River. He deeply hoped to be called back by the people to take up the position of the President. But, he took no measures towards it. He knew that the people wished for his return when the nation went into chaos. Yet, he waited for the people to call him back. It could also be said that his initial hope of the people to support him in his presidency was the cause of his sufferings. When he gave up his position as the President, he hoped to be elected back into power.

It was in vain, as a vast majority voted against him. Further, he also caused the citizens of the state to suffer in the hope of his return. Though he did not directly cause the suffering of the people, he was partly responsible for it. The people on their part did not do the right thing of calling him back but rather hoped for his return.

Hope and Psyche

The psyche of the Colonel in *No One Writes to the Colonel* is highly influenced by the hope that lies within him. The dire straits that he traverses do not seem to affect his state of mind. He was definitely frustrated at the state of affairs in his country. Yet, it did not affect his psyche as he was propelled forward by the hope of betterment in circumstances.

His pride is another evidence for this. Though he and his wife were on the verge of starvation, he would not let anyone know of his poverty, nor did he expect anyone to help him out. It was all based on his hope of overcoming his predicament. Therefore, it is clear that hope has definitely impacted his psyche and made his inner self strong enough to face his difficulties.

In the novel *Of Love and Other Demons*, Sierra Maria is the twelve-year-old daughter of the Marquis and his wife Bernarda. Her hair has never been trimmed, and was dedicated to the holy people, as she was born with the umbilical cord knotted around her neck. She was raised by the slaves, conversant in different African dialects, and acquainted with the traditions. As the book begins, she is nibbled by a raging canine.

Despite the fact that she gives no indications of rabies, she is made to undergo various healing strategies, which were nothing short of torment. She is shipped off to the community of Santa Clara to get an expulsion, which many individuals have passed on from. She gets consideration from a cleric, Father Cayetano, who is thoughtful to her and at first accepts she did need not an exorcism. Father Cayetano becomes hopelessly enamoured with Sierva Maria and professes her his adoration; before long he starts visiting Sierva in her cell covertly, ascending from the sewer. They eat, rest, and discuss verse together, despite the fact that it does not create the impression that they are physically involved.

Later Father Cayetano is sent away to an untouchable medical clinic where he desires to get the infection yet never does. Sierva Maria meanwhile is last called to be exorcized and she in the passes away "of love" pondering where Father Cayetano is and subsequent to having her hair cropped. After her demise, her hair mystically comes back on her skull.

> "*"Aren't you afraid you will be damned?"*
>
> *"I believe I already am, but not by the Holy Spirit," said Delaura without alarm. "I have always believed He attributes more importance to love than to faith." (OLOD, 135)*"

Aureliano Babilonia in *One Hundred Years of Solitude* is another example of the effect of hope on the psyche. He was brought up by his grandmother hidden from the society disguised as Aureliano II. After the death of his grandmother, he introduces himself to the society and tries to adjust to social life. But, he soon suffers set in life with the death of Amaranta Ursula and his child. Thus, he is forced to withdraw himself back to the old study of Melquiades. When he decoded the manuscript and understood the fate of Macondo and its residents, he calmly embraced it. This can be seen as an act of hopelessness. When he learned the future and was confirmed of its authenticity, he lost all hope and this impacted his psyche. The strange calmness with which he let himself be swept away by the storm is definite proof of his surrender and acceptance of the impending fate.

> "*Before reaching the final line, however, he had already understood that he would never leave that room, for it was foreseen that the city of mirrors (or mirages) would be wiped out by the wind and exiled from the memory of men at the precise moment when Aureliano Babilonia would finish deciphering the parchments... (OHYS, 422)*"

The mental health of the General in *TheGeneralinHisLabyrinth*has taken a serious blow in the absence of hope. He was initially hopeful when he resigned from the position of the President. But, when the people rejoiced at his failure and decision to flee, he lost the tiny sliver of hope. Further, the hateful graffiti and vandalism towards him trigger the collapse of his mental health. His perceived illnesses had all been minor discomforts but once his hope was lost, he believed himself to be a severely sick person. This ultimately led to the failure of his physical health too. Therefore, the hopelessness affected his psyche and it in turn worsened his sickness and consequently caused his death.

Conclusion

Hope is the quality of mind to expect positive results or outcome in any particular situation. It is featured as a prominent theme in the works of Garcia Marquez. C.R. Snyder's Hope Theory is used in this chapter to analyse the outcome of hope harboured by the characters of the select works. As per Snyder's theory, the presence and absence of hope is the major factor that decides the outcome of a venture. Having high hope makes a person a better achiever as opposed to a person with less hope. This chapter focuses on various aspects of hope and how it impacts a particular character. The aspects discussed are self-motivation through hope, hope in love and relationship, losing hope and failing, suffering in hope, and hope and psyche.

The study has found that most characters in these works are highly hopeful in their lives. While some of them put in serious effort to achieve the objectives with a positive feeling of the possibility of succeeding, other characters mere hope and lie in wait of their desires coming true. The first group of characters end up succeed in their mission whereas the latter group suffer failure or even worse lose their lives.

CHAPTER FIVE

ILLNESS: COMBATING AND SURVIVING

"Health is not valued till sickness comes." - Thomas Fuller

Introduction

A sickness is a particular strange condition that unfavourably impacts the development or capacity of all or part of an animal, and that is not a result of any unexpected external injury. Afflictions are habitually known to be infirmities that are connected with unequivocal after-effects and signs. An infection may be achieved by external variables like microorganisms or by inside dysfunctions. For example, inside dysfunctions of the safe structure can make many disorders, including various sorts of immunodeficiency, hypersensitivity, allergies and autoimmune disorders.

In individuals, ailment is commonly used even more completely to imply any condition that causes torture, brokenness, inconvenience, social issues, or end of the individual troubled or near issues for those in contact with the person. In this greater sense, it a portion of the time consolidates wounds, handicaps, wrecks, messes, defilements, bound secondary effects, degenerate approaches to acting, and unusual assortments of plan and capacity, while in various settings and for various purposes these may be seen as noticeable orders. Ailments can impact people really, yet furthermore mentally, as contracting and living with a disease can change the influenced person's perspective on life.

Death resulting from sickness is called death by natural causes. There are four essential sorts of disease: compelling contaminations, insufficiency ailments, acquired diseases (counting both genetic diseases and non-inherited inborn diseases), and physiological sicknesses. Ailments can in like manner be assembled in substitute ways, for instance, communicable versus non-adaptable afflictions. The deadliest afflictions in individuals are coronary conductor disease (circulatory system obstacle), followed by cerebrovascular disorder and lower respiratory defilements. In made countries, the diseases that cause the most problem overall are neuropsychiatric conditions, similar to wretchedness and anxiety.

The study of infection is called pathology, which incorporates the investigation of etiology, or cause. Generally speaking, terms, for example, infection, jumble, dismalness, ailment and disease are utilized reciprocally; notwithstanding, there are circumstances when explicit terms are thought of as ideal.

The term infection widely insinuates any condition that weakens the customary working of the body. Consequently, sicknesses are connected with separating of the body's overall homeostatic cycles. Routinely, the term is used to imply unequivocally to overpowering ailments, which are clinically clear disorders that result from the presence of pathogenic microbial subject matter experts, including diseases, microorganisms, developments, protozoa, multi-cell living things, and uncommon proteins known as prions. A defilement or colonization that does not and would not convey clinically clear impedance of commonplace working, similar to the presence of the regular microorganisms and yeasts in the stomach, or of an explorer contamination, is not seen as a sickness. Then again, a infection that is asymptomatic during its agonizing period, but expected to make incidental effects later, is regularly seen as a disease. Non-compelling ailments are any leftover contaminations, including most sorts of threatening development, coronary disease, and genetic affliction.

An acquired sickness is one that started sooner or later during one's lifetime, instead of illness that was at that point present upon entering the world, which is intrinsic infection. Procured recommends got through infection, however it essentially implies obtained after birth. It could likewise infer auxiliary sickness, however procured infection can be essential illness. An intense illness is one of a transient sort (intense); the term some of the time likewise hints a fulminant nature.

An idiopathic illness has an obscure reason or source. As clinical science has progressed, numerous sicknesses with completely obscure causes have had a few parts of their sources made sense of and in this manner shed their idiopathic status. For instance, when microbes were found, it became realized that they were a reason for contamination, however specific microorganisms and sicknesses had not been connected. In another model, it is realized that autoimmunity is the reason for certain types of diabetes mellitus type 1, despite the fact that the specific sub-atomic pathways by which it works are not yet perceived. It is likewise considered normal to realize specific elements are related with specific infections; in any case, affiliation and causality are two altogether different peculiarities, as a third reason may be creating the illness, as well as a related peculiarity. Illnesses that cannot be full cured, incurable illnesses are not really fatal sicknesses, and in some cases an infection's side effects can be dealt with adequately for the illness to no affect personal satisfaction.

A primary disease is an infection that is because of an underlying driver of sickness, rather than secondary disease, which is a sequela, or entanglement that is brought about by the primary disease. For instance, a typical virus is a primary disease, where rhinitis is a potential secondary disease, or sequela. A specialist should figure out what primary disease, a cold or bacterial contamination, is causing a patient's optional rhinitis while choosing whether or not to endorse anti-toxins. A secondary disease is an infection that is a sequela or confusion of an earlier, causal illness, which is alluded to as the primary disease or just the hidden reason (main driver). For instance, a bacterial disease can be primary, wherein a sound individual is presented to a bacterium and becomes contaminated, or it very well may be secondary to an primary driver, that inclines the body toward contamination. For instance, a primary viral disease that debilitates the safe framework could prompt a secondary bacterial contamination. Likewise, a primary burn that makes a painful injury could give a passage highlight microbes, and lead to a secondary bacterial disease. A fatal illness is one that is supposed to have the unavoidable consequence of death. Beforehand, AIDS was a fatal sickness; it is currently incurable, yet can be overseen endlessly utilizing drugs.

The terms ailment and disorder are both for the most part utilized as equivalent words for sickness; be that as it may, the term ailment is incidentally used to allude explicitly to the patient's very own insight of their infection. In this model, it is feasible for an individual to have a sickness without being sick (to have an impartially determinable, yet asymptomatic, ailment, like a subclinical contamination, or to have a clinically clear actual hindrance however not feel debilitated or upset by it), and to be sick without being unhealthy, (for example, when an individual sees a typical encounter as an ailment, or medicalizes a non-illness circumstance in their life - for instance, an individual who feels unwell because of shame, and who understands those sentiments as disorder as opposed to ordinary feelings). Side effects of disease are many times not straightforwardly the consequence of contamination, but rather an assortment of developed reactions - disorder conduct by the body - that helps clear contamination and advance recuperation. Such parts of sickness can incorporate laziness, discouragement, loss of craving, tiredness, hyperalgesia, and failure to focus.

A disorder is a useful irregularity or unsettling influence. Clinical problems can be arranged into mental issues, actual problems, hereditary issues, profound and social issues, and utilitarian issues. The term problem is many times thought about additional worth nonpartisan and less trashing than the terms sickness or disease, and accordingly is favoured phrasing in certain conditions. In emotional well-being, the term mental turmoil is utilized as an approach to recognizing the mind boggling collaboration of natural, social, and mental variables in mental circumstances; in any case, the term problem is likewise utilized in numerous different areas of medication, basically to distinguish actual problems that are not brought about by irresistible organic entities, like metabolic problems.

An illness is an extensive term that integrates all diseases, wounds, wrecks, or non-pathologic condition that consistently seeks clinical treatment, similar to pregnancy or labour. While the term generally consolidates mental ailments, in specific settings the term is used unequivocally to mean any disorder, injury, or disease beside broken ways of behaving. The Diagnostic and Statistical Manual of Mental Disorders (DSM), the comprehensively used mental manual that portrays each and every psychological issue, uses the term general illness to imply all ailments, sicknesses, and wounds beside mental issues. This utilization is moreover commonly tracked down in the psychological composition. Some medical care techniques in like manner portray an illness as any affliction, injury, or contamination except for mental sicknesses.

As it is more worth impartial than terms like illness, the term ailment is once in a while liked by individuals with medical problems that they don't consider harmful. Then again, by accentuating the clinical idea of the condition, this term is some of the time dismissed, for example, by defenders of the chemical imbalance privileges development. The term ailment is likewise an equivalent word for clinical state, in which case it portrays a singular patient's present status from a clinical outlook. This use shows up in proclamations that portray a patient as being in basic condition, for instance.

This part endeavours to investigate the portrayal of ailment, both physical and mental, which are integral to crafted by Garcia Marquez. An extensive variety of physical and dysfunctional behaviour are visible in the works of Garcia Marquez. These ailments are crucial for the advancement of the plots.

Societal Attitude towards Illness

Illness presents the social legitimization of specific advantages, for example, ailment benefits, work evasion, and being cared for by others. The individual who is debilitated takes on a social job called the wiped out job. An individual who answers a feared sickness, for example, malignant growth, in a socially OK design might be freely and secretly regarded with higher economic wellbeing. As a trade-off for these advantages, the debilitated individual is committed to look for treatment and attempt to turn out to be well again. As an examination, consider pregnancy, which isn't deciphered as an illness or disorder, regardless of whether the mother and child may both advantage from clinical consideration.

Most religions award special cases from strict obligations to individuals who are debilitated. For instance, one whose life would be imperiled by fasting on Yom Kippur or during Ramadan is absolved from the necessity, or even taboo from taking an interest. Individuals who are wiped out are likewise excluded from social obligations. For instance, infirmity is the sole acceptable justification behind an American to decline a solicitation to the White House. The distinguishing proof of a condition as an illness, as opposed to as essentially a variety of human construction or capability, can have huge social or monetary ramifications.

The disputable acknowledgment of sicknesses like repetitive stress injury (RSI) and post-traumatic stress disorder (PTSD) has had various positive and adverse consequences on the monetary and different obligations of states, companies, and establishments towards people, as well as on the actual people. The social ramifications of survey maturing as a sickness could be significant, however this grouping isn't yet inescapable.

Lepers were individuals who were generally evaded in light of the fact that they had an irresistible illness, and the expression "leper" actually brings out friendly disgrace. Feeling of dread toward sickness can in any case be a boundless social peculiarity, however not all illnesses bring out outrageous social disgrace.

Social standing and monetary status influence wellbeing. Sicknesses of neediness are infections that are related with destitution and low societal position; illnesses of abundance are sicknesses that are related with high friendly and monetary status. The relation of infections with conditions shifts as indicated by time, spot, and innovation. A few sicknesses, for example, diabetes mellitus, might be related with both destitution (unhealthy food decisions) and riches (long life expectancy and inactive ways of life), through various systems. The term way of life infections alludes to illnesses related with life span and that are more normal among more seasoned individuals. For instance, malignant growth is undeniably more normal in social orders in which most individuals live until they arrive at the age of eighty than in social orders wherein most individuals pass away before they arrive at the age of fifty.

Of Love and Other Demons portrays the story of twelve-year old Sierva Maria. In this novel, Sierva is depicted as a girl generally neglected by her father, the Marquis. She was raised by the slaves of the household and thus she became quite fluent in many African languages and followed their 'pagan' traditions and cultural tenets. She was often found with braided hair and adorning tribal stone necklaces. Altogether she was a misfit in her own class while being a great fit among the slaves.

Sierva Maria was always an attention grabber due to her non-conformist behaviour. She was always a topic of great interest to the society. But, this changes shape when she is bitten by a rabid dog and shows signs of illness. From then on, she is pitied by the residents of the town for her illness, though it seems to be only a fever. But, once the news of her being bitten by the dog and her illness reaches the Bishop, this pity is replaced with fear and panic. The bishop believes that she is possessed by some demonic spirits and her illness is only an outward symptom of the possession. The townspeople accept the bishop's words for truth and believe that she is indeed possessed.

While considering her father, the Marquis, his attitude towards her changes, after she was bitten by the dog and fell ill. He had until then ignored her and her well-being. But, when she falls ill, he is genuinely concerned about her and summons the doctor. It is unclear what brings about this change in attitude. One is left wondering, if it was his fatherly love that awakes in him when he finds her sick. Or, it could be the fear of himself or his whole estate contracting the illness. However, it must be noted that he showed genuine concern about her illness.

The epidemic of cholera, which becomes the canvas for the novel *Love in the Time of Cholera,* has wide spread effect on the social life in the novel. The epidemic brought to light the disparities in the lifestyles of the various classes in the society. The deplorable living conditions of the economically poor classes caused the epidemic to spread rapidly among them. While the wealthy class too got affected by the disease, the spread was not as drastic as it was in the lower strata. Even the civic authorities did not care to bring changes to the living conditions. They lacked even basic infrastructure like covered sewage system and septic tanks.

When Dr. Urbino brought this matter to the notice of the authorities, they decide to take necessary steps to build drainage systems and proper toilets. But the intention was not to keep the poor people safe but to prevent the spread of the disease in the society and thereby keeping the wealthy people safe. This makes one question the value of a person's life. One is left wondering whether money and status adds more value to an individual. The people living in the slums where not bothered by their living conditions as they did not have the education to understand the consequences of their nasty abodes and dirty public utilities.

Furthermore, people in general were quite suspicious and cautious of those affected by cholera. Rather than helping them, most people preferred to abandon them or isolate them out of fear of infection. This is proved by the scene where the captain of the river boat is asked to raise the yellow flag, which was a sign of cholera on board, so that no port would admit them nor would anybody board the ship. Additionally, the disease also caused the society to crumble and start a civil war when the government was unable to protect the citizens from the disease or provide them with basic necessities.

Combating Illness

The novel *One Hundred Years of Solitude* presents a variety of illnesses, both individual illnesses and mass illnesses. The prominent ones among these are the plagues of insomnia, amnesia and insanity. Insomnia starts as a mass illness among the residents of the village and everyone suffers from it, while nobody seems to be adversely affected by it after effects.

Jose Arcadia Buendia, along with the entire village, faces a period of Insomnia. He is unable to sleep yet is completely unaffected by it he finds it a boon and goes on with his daily routine. He believes this illness has given him more time to involve in his passions and vocation. The availability of more time seems to be a good prospect initially, but as time progresses the flip side of it would reveal itself. It could lead to a world where people would have too much idle time in hand and feel bored with their life. This could in turn cause the moral fabric of the society to collapse as every individual seeks out their preferred method to utilize the excess time at hand.

Amnesia kicks in as a mass illness in the whole village with minor forgetfulness of names of things. In the initial stage, they forget trivial things like this but later move to serious stages where they even find it difficult to remember what is what and how things are done. With this, they start losing their grip on reality and daily life. Then, Jose Arcadio Buendia comes up with a brilliant plan. He starts pasting labels on things. These labels contain the name and brief description of what is to be done with the respective thing.

An example of this is the tag tied around the neck of the cow which said that it was a cow and it needed to be milked twice a day. This soon becomes a regular practice among the villagers and everyone starts following it. This way they are able to fight off the illness and consequent difficulties in their daily lives. It was through the inquisitiveness of Jose Arcadio Buendia that people noticed the illness and overcame the illness until everyone was cured of it. Jose Arcadio Buendia had always been this way and was a pioneer in all spheres of life.

The very nature of Jose Arcadio Buendia leads him down the path of insanity. His curious and inquisitive nature led him to pursue the studies of Melquiades and ultimately lose his mind within the corridors of mysterious knowledge. His behaviour became exceptionally erratic. One day, he turned violent and self destructive. As a result, he is restrained by many men and bound to a tree where he remained till the end of his life. It could be speculated that Jose Arcadio Buendia's whole life was a struggle against insanity to which he finally succumbed. His fits of rage, mysterious yet eccentric nature are all signs of insanity that he exhibited throughout. But, he was able to keep it together until old-age where he went insane.

In *Love in the Time of Cholera*, there appears to be two serious illnesses. One is Cholera itself while the other is the metaphorical illness of love. While taking love into consideration Florentino Ariza the protagonist is the one affected by the illness. All the physical symptoms that he exhibit are suggestive of the emotion of love being similar to a disease. As an immediate reaction of love he almost faints, feels nauseous and tired. It almost resembles the onslaught of Cholera but later his uncle diagnoses and reveals that it is not cholera. The illness of love turns out to be as much physical as it is mental. The severity of his love and its effects on his mind manifest the physical illness. Later the sole symptom is his experiencing physical pain. He overcomes this through his countless affairs with other women.

The second illness to be discussed is the epidemic of cholera. The entire set of characters in the novel face and combat this illness on a personal level, while Dr. Urbino sets out to fight the illness not for himself but for the entire city. He had personally faced the tragedy of illness when his father passed away but he takes it up as a mission in life to fight illnesses and give a healthy life to people.

Dr. Urbino is the first person to investigate the possible reasons for the spread of Cholera. Upon his investigation he finds that the living conditions of the highly affected areas are unsanitary and lack even basic infrastructure but nobody had thought of this to be the reason for the epidemic. Even the residents of these areas who were primarily, working class people, nor the city administration had thought of these conditions until the he brought it to their notice and pointed it out as a major cause of the epidemic. At his behest the city administration starts renovating the area and provides them better infrastructure and drainage system not for the betterment of the lives of the working class people but for protecting the upper class from the epidemic. Through his fight against the epidemic Dr. Urbino becomes a national hero and, in all means, a true saviour of the people.

When it comes to Florentino and Fermina, their fight against cholera was to attain their hearts' desire. They fell in love with each other at a time when the city was ravished by the epidemic of Cholera. When the world around them was struggling to survive, they both forget everything about the hardships of the epidemic along with the civil war which ran parallel to it, and moved into a separate world of their own which is free from all fears and troubles. Staying at a safe distance from each other, they exchange love letters and love poems. Their relationship grows stronger despite the physical separation until the day Fermina returned from the ranch and calls off their affair.

Half a century later, they rekindle their relationship when Florentino once again professes his love for her after the death of a husband. Here, their love is allowed to blossom with the help of the fear of Cholera. Florentino and Fermina undertake a voyage in the river boat and, to prohibit others entry to the boat, Florentino asks the captain to raise the yellow flag as a warning of Cholera on-board the ship. This way they make use of the epidemic to their benefit.

In *TheGeneralintheLabyrinth,*the General is affected by a strange and mysterious illness which is never diagnosed by anyone. The General, despite being in his forties, faces many conditions which are common in old-age. He appears to be fighting this illness all through the course of the novel and finally succumbed to it. As he finds it weakness in character to fall sick and consult a doctor, the General devices very strange and unique remedies to keep his illness under the check. His daily bath routine is an example. He immerses himself in a bathtub with hot aromatic water mixed with numerous flowers and salts. His inability to sleep was kept under control with the help of Manuela Saenz who visited him secretly every night and read out to him. The General believed it a mental weakness to consult a doctor. He had never once sought the help of a doctor until near the end of the novel where he was physically extremely weak. Even then, the doctors were unable to find valid cause for his illness. It could be assumed that his ailment was tuberculosis but there was no evidence to prove it.

*OfLoveandOtherDemons*depicts the struggle of Sierva Maria against her alleged illnesses. The illnesses alleged upon her are rabies infection and demonic possession. Both of these allegations prove to be false to the readers while the other characters fail to see the light of the day after. After she was bitten by a stray dog, she exhibits mild symptoms of infection and soon the dog that bit her dies of rabies. This strikes fear in the minds of her father and others. She is then treated for rabies which apparently she had not contracted. She struggles to remain sane throughout this ordeal. But her struggle comes to nought when the bishop falsely diagnoses her of demonic possession. She is helpless and unable to escape from the Bishop's allegation, yet she put up a fight. With the arrival of Father Cayetano Delaura, some hope enters a life. Once he showers his affection on her she lets her guard down, feeling protected by him.

This proved to be her doom as Delaura is overcome by his guilt and confesses the whole thing to the Bishop. As a penal action, Delaura is sent off to a hospital to care for lepers. With Delaura away from her, Sierva Maria finds herself defeated and is left with no more initiative to fight. Had she been left alone to fight for herself she would have had a better chance to succeed but the emotional support and attachment made her weak and defenseless. Soon afterwards, the bishop directly takes over her exorcism and Sierva Maria succumbs to have fate.

Meanwhile Delaura, who is sent away to care for lepers, too had reached the final mental state of Sierva Maria, as in, he had accepted his fate and wishes to get the illness from the hospital and write the major differences that can be seen among these two characters are their purpose in life and the way they approach the illness. Sierva Maria never steps back from the alleged illness, despite her helpless state but Delaura, who is brought into fight off the others' illness, lack the mental strength and gives up and ultimately wishes for death.

Love as an Illness

The foremost noticeable subject of the novel, *LoveintheTimeofCholera*, proposes that lovesickness could indeed be a physical ailment, a torment likened to cholera. The symptoms of lovesickness displayed by Florentino Ariza resemble those of cholera, persevering both physical and passionate torments as he yearns for his lady love. In the second chapter, the worry of rejection and being ignored by Fermina makes Florentino is severely ill. When his mother brings in his godfather, a practitioner of homeopathy, to examine him, Florentino's lovesickness is at first mistaken for cholera. Florentino's ailment, it very well may be contended, rises above the physical to the mental, for however his illness lies in his heart and in his stomach, he is impulsively fixated, and thusly emotionally upset.

Florentino's passionate torment is complicated by physical anguish after he spews upon eating blossoms and drinking cologne so that he may keep in mind Fermina's fragrance. The critical craving for death makes his physical torment appear to be a sign of cholera, the turmoil caused by adoration. As per Millington (2010), Garcia Marquez draws on the dignified and sentimental conventions which compare adoration to an affliction. Cholera is connected with the city's need of mindfulness of open wellbeing on a strict level. Yet on an idyllic level, the fevers of cholera and the sufferings of adoration entwine reliably. Cholera and love permeates the novel on an equal level.

To put it plainly, cholera is not merely a metaphoric allusion. Rather, it symbolises a kind of encompassing air of mortality, malady and festering that reminds of the brevity of life, and simultaneously, of love's direness. The cholera allegory has succeeded in its numerous employments and hence depicts a characteristic juxtaposition of death and love. Therefore, though the allusion of cholera is used for setting the context and bringing the emotional status of the characters to the forefront, it does hold water. Death and love intertwine in the novel.

The death scene of Dr. Urbino, his dying thoughts and his last words are further testaments of the merger of love and death. His fear of death and aging, which is frequently featured in the novel is nowhere in his mind right before death. He rather felt the pain of leaving his wife and moving on.

> "*He recognized her despite the uproar, through his tears of unrepeatable sorrow at dying without her, ... he managed to say to her with his last breath:*
> *"Only God knows how much I loved you." (LTC, 32)*"

The subject of affection as a plague features in the concluding chapter of the novel, wherein Florentino orders the Captain of the boat on which he and Fermina are on board to declare, that there is an case of cholera on the boat. In spite of the fact that there is no instance of cholera on board the boat, the case is not completely erroneous, for Florentino has been stricken by a persistent obsession for Fermina since more than half a decade ago when she rebuffed his advances in the Arcade of the Scribes. His obsession has endured similar to a dangerous plague of cholera, for Florentino is in a true sense tormented by adoration.

The novel depicts the spirit torturing impact of the lethal sickness called love. *Love in the Time of Cholera* narrates the immortal adoration of Florentino Ariza who, having desired

Fermina Daza in her young age, subtly reveres her for more than fifty one years till the day he attained her. The principal theme of the novel is the long lasting dedication of Florentino Ariza to Fermina Dasa. His adoration for her resembles severe illness which develops with time with no regular outlet and no alleviation. The timeline of the novel ranges from the close of the nineteenth century to the initial decades of the twentieth century. Marquez surrounds his novels within images of death. Blending a touch of noteworthy subtleties, he depicts the cholera epidemic that plagued Paris in the year 1892. The epidemic rapidly travelled beyond the North Atlantic and reached the Columbian coast.

Through this similitude, Garcia Marquez connects the novel to its transient and, surprisingly, political setting. The episode of cholera which handily flourished in urban communities and towns tormented by ill-equipped infrastructure and poverty remains as major areas of strength for Florentino Ariza's tormented love. The setting of an infected world is a fundamental part of the novel in light of the fact that Marquez frequently suggests the possibility that love has same side effects as a fatal illness. Cholera functions as a strong representation in the original that depicts the generally long-lasting, quick and terrible impacts of the destructive illness of love.

The perusers are transported to a period in the past to an account of love at first sight. Florentino Ariza and Fermina Daza are both eighteen and thirteen years of age respectively, when they first see each other. It was then the long and torturing course of stalling and the ceaseless impacts of the infection called love commenced. A single glance from Fermina starts the disturbance of adoration that requires more than five decades to reach its climax. When Florentino waits for Fermina Daza to the reply of his first love letter, he exhibits symptoms of tiredness which his mom mistakes for Cholera. During the same time, Florentino loses hunger and his voice and goes through the whole evening thrashing around is his bed. His torment is worsened by diarrhoea and nausea.

> "*After Florentino Ariza saw her for the first time, his mother knew before he told her because he lost his voice and his appetite and spent the entire night tossing and turning in his bed. But when he began to wait for the answer to his first letter, his anguish was complicated by diarrhea and green vomit, he became disoriented and suffered from sudden fainting spells, and his mother was terrified because his condition did not resemble the turmoil of love so much as the devastation of cholera. (LTC, 43)*"

Of Love and Other Demons portray another dimension of love that springs out of the dire circumstances that Sierva Maria gets trapped in. Here, it was the shear hopelessness that reinforced the relationship between Sierva Maria and Delaura. This love later became the illness that caused her death. Sierva Maria held on to her dear life despite the torture and exorcism. Love was her lifeline and the moment it was cut she gave up her fight and died. She was safe as long as she was away from love. She had lived all her life without love and affection. Even as a child, she survived the lack of love and still turned out to be strong individual. But once she was introduced to love, her downfall commenced. Love made her dependant on it and then caused her death as it left her.

The same is the case with her mother, Bernarda. Her extramarital relationship with Judas is points out the addictive nature of love on both metaphoric and literal levels as the latter introduced her to a world of hallucinogens and intoxication. Additionally, Sierva's admirer Father Delaura happened to be addicted to love poems and the idea of love. It can be said that he was in the wrong vocation with a mind so keen on romantic love. Therefore, it could also be said that he was affected by the illness called love.

Conquering Illness through Hope and Individualism

In the novel *Love in the Time of Cholera,* illness, aging and death are always looming in the lives of the characters. The novel opens with the description of the dead body of Jeremiah de Saint Amour.

It is found that Saint-Amour had killed himself. He had previously made all preparations for his death. He was crippled from waist below and had lived in that debilitating state for quite a long time. He had decided long ago that he would end his life at a particular age. His decision was based on his desire to live on his own terms and independently. He was able to overcome his physical disability to a great extend but he knew that one day he would be unable to do so as he ages. Therefore, he made the decision not to live long enough to reach that state.

In this case, his decision to end his life cannot be seen as a sign of weakness or cowardice. It was indeed a strong and individualistic act on his part. Yet, he chose to accept death instead of facing the possible troubles in future. Therefore, it cannot be considered as a positive individualistic action. Though, he overcame the difficulties, of oldage and related illness coupled with his difficulties through his own ways, ultimately the loss was his. The victory over illness is definitely overshadowed by his death. Hence, he could not be taken as a person who achieved success through individualism.

Sierva Maria in *Of Love and Other Demons* was always perceived as a threat to faith by the Bishop. Her dressing style, her stone necklaces and tribal jewellery, her following African religious practices and speaking African dialects were seen as signs of demonic possession. Apparently, he feared that his authority over the townspeople would be challenged if Sierva Maria continued to follow her way of life. As the religious head of the town, he had absolute control over the people and their religious liberty. Therefore, he took it upon himself to keep the people strongly rooted in their faith.

The attack of the rabid dog presented him the opportunity he had been longing for. Thus, he seized the opportunity to take her in and bring her back to the faith and, in turn, stabilized his own position and the faith of the people. He then brands her as possessed by evil spirits and orders an exorcism. He does not even consider the fact that many people have lost their lives as a result of it. His actions should be considered as the desperate steps of a power crazy person to retain his authority.

The relationship between Delaura and Sierva Maria takes place due to her illness and consequent isolation. It is found that Delaura entices her with love poems and soothing words. He offers her companionship at her time of isolation. Despite his vow of celibacy, Delaura seduces the girl and continues to have relationship with her until he finally breaks down and confesses to the Bishop. It needs to be questioned whether this relationship would have happened if Sierva Maria was not bitten by the dog and had not fallen sick. The answer is an emphatic 'no'. But, in the novel, it happens and the girl is not in any position to resist or expose him. Though, he does not physically force her, he ignores the fact that she is only a child. Therefore, this relationship could be considered a rape, which was committed by taking advantage of her alleged illness and confinement.

In both these cases, the alleged illness of Sierva Maria was used as a means of demonizing, ostracizing, institutionalizing, exploiting and, finally, eliminating her. The Bishop and Delaura twist and turn the opportunity to suit their needs. Hence, it could be said that they use the illness to their advantage.

The diseases depicted in *One Hundred Years of Solitude* and the reactions of the characters towards them are undoubtedly some of the most innovative ways to overcome diseases. Moreover the kind of positivity and the presence of mind displayed by the characters are genuinely appreciable. It should be noted that these characters are isolated in a village with no adequate medical facilities or government authorities to look into the matters. Yet, they find hope and positive outcomes to the strange and magical diseases they encounter.

Initially when the village is affected by insomnia, which is generally considered the worst condition one could go through. Jose Arcadio Buendia found it to be a blessing in disguise. He believed that it could be a boon as it would provide everyone with more time to involve in their professional or passionate vocations and thus be more productive. "If we don't ever sleep again, so much the better," Jose Arcadio Buendia said in good humor. "That way we can get more out of life." (*OHYS*, 28) It is definitely the most positive way to look at a serious medical condition. Through this he was able to remove the fear from the minds of the people and keep them enthusiastic.

As a later wave of insomnia, the villagers were affected by collective amnesia. In this case they started forgetting trivial things such as name of things. As the illness progressed, they started forgetting even more important things such as how things were used. They even forgot what a cow was and in what manner it was useful. Even in this case, Jose Arcadio Buendia came to the rescue. He noticed the disease in its onslaught and came up with a genius way to defeat it. He decided to tie tags on everything that was useful. The tags had information such as the name of the thing and how it was to be used. The tag in the neck of the cow mentioned that it was a cow and had to be milked twice a day.

Illness and Psyche

Health psychology is the forte that centres on the impact of physiology, psychology, conduct, and societal variables on wellbeing and sickness. Various terms such as medical psychology and behavioural medical therapy are in some cases utilized in its stead. Wellbeing and sickness are impacted by a wide assortment of variables.

Although infectious and genetic sicknesses are common, numerous behavioural and mental variables can affect general health and other therapeutic conditions.

The discipline of health psychology primarily aims at advancing physical wellbeing as well as the anticipation and treatment of infection and sickness. Practitioners of health psychology also focus on analysing how individuals respond to, manage with, and recuperate from sickness. Another group of practitioners focus on the creation of a better framework for healthcare and revamping the government's approach to healthcare.

Conceived in the 1970s, it was developed to tend to the quick changes within the field of healthcare. Owing to the lack of proper sanitation facilities and rampant epidemics, life expectancy had been much lower during that period. At present, the average lifespan in the United States is near eighty years and the serious lifestyle illnesses are the major cause of death. Health psychology studies these changes in wellbeing. Practitioners of health psychology believe they can assist individuals to live happier and healthier lives, by analysing the behavioural patterns that cause illness and mortality.

In *Love in the Time of Cholera*, ailment, maturing and death are continuously approaching the lives of the heroes. The portrayal of Jeremiah de Saint-Amour the Antillean refugee's dead body, to examine which his companion Dr. Juvenal Urbino is summoned to look at, kick-starts the novel. After seeing the mortal remains of his friend, Dr. Urbino is reminded of his own mortality. Throughout the novel, different characters encounter similae situations of realisation. In fact, in spite of the fact that individuals like Dr. Urbino play an imperative part in ridding society of perilous infections like cholera, the method by which they all accustom themself with their own mortality is highly individualized. All the major characters, be it Florentino Ariza, Fermina Daza, and her husband Dr. Urbino, realise that they have to come to terms with their aging process. In any case, rather than giving in to acquiescence, Fermina and Florentino discover a different path: devoting their last years to fill their lifes as much love and happiness as they possibly can.

The book proposes that no hope or love is wasted if it lightens the mood and brightens the hearts of the people till the approach of death. As a well educated physician, Dr. Juvenal Urbino holds the view that the lives of the people and the society in general can be highly benefitted by advanced scientific and medical developments. He noticed that certain local practices have caused the worsening of cholera spread, when he arrived from Paris. The superstition of drinking water that was infested with water worms was an appalling sight for him. Despite, its harmful effects the people still followed the practice. Hernia in the scrotum which was a serious medical condition was considered a sign of virility.

Finally, although cholera infection knew no boundaries of race, status or wealth, the mortality rate due to cholera was discovered to be greater in the slums where poor and black people lived owing to the lack of covered drainage system and septic tanks. Mindful of these clinical and social issues, Dr. Juvenal Urbino never permits himself to capitulate to the sadness of the circumstances; rather he endeavours to track down arrangements. He battles to fabricate a shut sewage framework, to persuade individuals not to discard squander anyplace, and to move the slaughterhouse farther from where individuals reside and dine. These imaginative techniques assume a significant part in forestalling another flare-up of cholera in the city, showing that society can advance and shield itself from controllable illnesses, as opposed to simply tolerating death as destiny.

Aside from social development, on an individual level Dr. Urbino and different characters are compelled to acknowledge that there is one thing in human existence that even all that clinical changes cannot conquer aging and mortality. Time elapsing incites ghastliness and frenzy in different characters. Florentino sees the attacks of time not in his own life, but rather in those of others. Specifically, he is stunned to see Fermina Daza nearly stumble on strides openly while clutching her better half. At that time, Florentino understands that what panics him more than anything else is growing old, which could drive him to depend on someone else for help, in the way that Fermina and her better half rely upon one another to make due. Despite the fact that characters attempt to guard themselves against aging, their endeavours are generally purposeless. Most characters in the novel show a mentality toward aging that is set apart by dread and disgrace, believing advanced age to embarrass. Jeremiah de Saint-Amour takes an especially uncommon measure to forestall aging and related illnesses: self destruction. Dr. Urbino does not attempt suicide, yet covertly takes different drugs to forestall specific issues related with aging, for example, dizziness and sleep related issues. Essentially, Florentino is embarrassed to become hairless and to need to supplant his teeth. As opposed to either tolerating advanced age as an unavoidable piece of life or attempting to better themselves, these characters attempt to no end to disregard and cover their concerns.

Eventually, be that as it may, anything precautionary measures or sentiments characters could have about aging and passing on, they come to realise that they have zero power over how and when they draw their last breathe. Dr. Juvenal Urbino falls to his death while climbing a tree in an attempt to get his pet parrot that had escaped. He demise stands out obviously from his standing as a serious, honourable man for its dark humour. This shows that passing is flighty and astounding and, hence, that stressing over it has no influence on its result.

Thus, the sole way to deal with for aging and demise is to go up against this point of life head-on and make the best of whatever time one has got on Earth. Florentino and Fermina understand that disgrace adds nothing certain to their lives. Despite the fact that they are both apprehensive about the other finding their old body and their "sour smell of old age" (*LTC*, 217) while in bed, they eventually demonstrate tolerance towards one another's physical condition. Rather than thinking about that mature age is an impediment to their adoration, they acknowledge that they can now communicate emotions in another manner: through quiet, delicate demonstrations, in conflict with the enthusiastic intercourse and force of their young age.

Toward the close of the novel, apparently the cure for the unavoidable battles of ailment and maturing is to make the best of tough spots and appreciate life however much as could reasonably be expected. On the boat, when Florentino and Fermina are going to get back to port and the standard idea of their lives and, thusly, to the approach of their passing they choose to trust that "it is life, more than death, that has no limits." (*LTC*, 225) Instead of yielding to death, they turn the boat around, rejecting the truth of fatigue and flimsiness. Similarly as Dr. Urbino's obligation to prevention of illness advocates a hopeful and proactive point of view, their decision to continue to have fun underlines that passing is eventually beyond their control, but not their ability to partake in their own lives.

One Hundred Years of Solitude is the account of seven ages of the Buendia Family in the town of Macondo. The plot of the novel takes the reader through an array of illnesses which are fascinating and literal at the same time. The most striking of these are the episodes of Insomnia and selective amnesia that plagues the entire village. At a point of time the entire population of the village is unable to fall asleep. They roam around the village at night unable to sleep. Yet the people get accustomed to it and never feel the burden of it. They are rather happy of their situation as they believe they can make the best of their time. But they are unaware of the implications of the disease.

> "*"If we don't ever sleep again, so much the better," Jose Arcadio Buendia said in good humor. "That way we can get more out of life." ... finally the identity of people and even the awareness of his own being, until he sank into a kind of idiocy that had no past. (OHYS, 28)*"

The ultimate result that the people of the village are oblivious of is explained in the above quote. This leads the readers to the next disease in question. It is the case of dementia which is so acute that people forget even the names of things around them.

This gets even worse when they also forget what was to be done with the things around them. They even forget what a cow was and that it had to be milked every day. Finally, Jose Arcadio Buendia comes up with the idea of using labels on everything. Everything around the village had label attached to it. The labels contained the name of the thing or animal along with a small description of what was to be done with it. For instance, the cows' labels mentioned that it was a cow and that it had to be milked every day.

Insomnia and dementia are quite common diseases found among human beings but what makes these episodes interesting is the fact that the entire village suffers from the same disease at the same time. This seems impossible but impossible things were daily happenings in the village. Hence, it is never out of the logic of the readers.

Another incident which is quite similar to the mass dementia is the incident of selective amnesia experienced by the residents of the case of the banana massacre. Jose Arcadio Segundo is the only person who remembers the incident.

> "*At first it seemed that the machine guns were loaded with caps... No reaction was perceived...the compact crowd seemed petrified by an instantaneous invulnerability. Then a cry of death tore open the*
>
> *enchantment: 'Aaaagh mother'. A seismic voice, a volcanic breath, the roar of a cataclysm broke out in the centre of the crowd with a great potential of expansion.*
>
> *The people in front of Jose Aracadio Buendia... had been swept down by the wave of bullets.................................. systematically being cut off all round like an onion being peeled by the insatiable and methodical shears of the machine guns. (OHYS, 149 -150)*"

Such a gruesome incident never seems to exist in the memory of the villagers.

Despite Jose Arcadio Segundo's consistent effort no one remembers the incident once the evidence was washed off by the continuous five years of rain.

Remedios Moscote's influence on Colonel Aureliano is another instance to prove the influence of the psyche in generating an illness. Colonel Aureliano was unable to get her off of his mind and the feeling was as physical as mental.

> "*The image of Remedios, the magistrate's younger daughter, who, because of her age, could have been his daughter, kept paining him in some part of his body. It was*

> *a physical sensation that almost bothered him when he walked, like a pebble in his shoe. (OHYS 34)*"

Further, the sudden fit of asthma that he experienced in her presence also proves the ability of the psyche to induce a physical illness.

> "*Remedios went over and asked some questions about the fish that Aureliano could not answer because he was seized with a sudden attack of asthma. He wanted to stay beside that lily skin forever, beside those emerald eyes, close to that voice that called him "sir" with every question. (OHYS 37)*"

When Rebecca's anger crossed the limits and reached a physical level she exhibits weird behaviour bordering on insanity. Here, the extent of emotional turmoil causes it effects to transcend from mental to physical and further to a psychotic ultimately causing self harm to the affected individual.

> "*Mad with desperation, Rebecca got up in the middle of the night and ate handfuls of earth in the garden with a suicidal drive, weeping with pain ...of leaves and petals preserved in old books and the dried butterflies that turned to powder at the touch. (OHYS 38)*"

Of Love and Other Demons depict multiple kinds of diseases and a wide array of approaches towards diseases. Sometime in the colonial era, in a country along the Caribbean coast line lived Sierva Maria de Todos los Angeles aged twelve with her unconventional parents. Her father was the descendant of a family from the rotting aristocracy. Apparently, he was a frail man lacking good judgment. Her mother happened to be a cunning nymphomaniac who was addicted to fermented honey and cacao tablets. Sierva Maria was cared for by the household slaves and thus she absorbed their culture. She possessed lush copper-coloured hair and a propensity for lying, "she wouldn't tell the truth even by mistake" according to her mother. (*OLOD* 16) She was bitten by a rabid dog in the left ankle.

> "*An ash-gray dog with a white blaze on its forehead burst onto the rough terrain of the market on the first Sunday in December, knocked down tables of fried food, overturned Indians' stalls and lottery kiosks, and bit four people who happened to cross its path. (OLOD, 5)*"

Not long afterwards, the dog died of rabies. Despite everyone appearing to have his or her possess hypothesis, no one had a clear reason when bizarre behaviour is observed in Sierva Maria. The questions of whether the girl is displaying signs of rabies, whether she is possessed by a demon and so on linger in the minds of everyone around her.

The doctor Abrenuncio questions either conclusion. The scheming Bishop accepts the young lady may require a severe religious cleansing. Maybe Sierva Maria is essentially unpredictable or possibly indeed insane. She is institutionalised in the Santa Clara Convent ninety-three days after the attack of the rabid dog, where she was isolated in a cell.

Father Cayetano Delaura, the 36-year-old protege of the Bishop is tasked to explore the matter. The cleric is instantly charmed with the young lady. The priest is punished and consigned to caring for people affected by leprosy at a healing center, when the Bishop comes to know about the love affair between Cayetano Delaura's and Sierva Maria. Following this the Bishop himself assumes charge of performing the ceremony of cleansing on Sierva Maria. Before the sixth session, she was discovered "dead of love" (*OLOD* 147) in her bed.

The first aspect to be looked upon is the disease of fear that seems to cause all the troubles in the life of Sierva Maria. The psychological disease of fear, especially of the unknown makes the major characters stay away from Sierva. Her peculiar behaviour was the result of being raised by the slaves of the household, who were predominantly Africans. She was neglected by her parents and she adopted the cultural traits of those that cared for her. Therefore, she was demonised for being a white girl who exhibited African cultural traits. Similarly, when she is bitten by a rabid dog, the people are scared that she might contract rabies. Fortunately or unfortunately, she does not contract rabies, this surprises them and they react by ostracizing her. They fear that she is possessed by demonic spirits. This has always been the case with society. They turn to witch doctors and spells for diseases. In the case of Sierva Maria, not contracting a disease, when she was supposed to, caused all the trouble.

She is therefore sent off for "treatment" at an asylum. The treatment suggested by the fanatic Bishop is exorcism. The age old belief of discarding and hating foreignness is the reason behind this. This is also a kind of fear which springs from insecurity. The Bishop is insecure of his position and authority. He tries to secure it by invoking fear in the minds of the people.

There are different approaches to disease being portrayed in this novel. The most prominent ones are those of Sierva Maria and Cayetano. Sierva Maria accepts the disease in plain submission. She has always been secluded in her life and thus, the isolation due to her so called disease is of no significance to her. At the same time, she feels content in this state as she feels cared for. She had never experienced love in her life. But, while she is in the cell, she feels loved by Cayetano. This is the sole comfort that she needs to overcome her desolate state.

Turning over to the case of Cayetano, he is sent away to a hospital for lepers after he confesses his relationship with Sierva Maria. There, he longs for the disease. It is more like a suicidal thought. He wishes that he gets the disease and die. He finds disease as salvation. He wants to be absolved from his sin. The method that he chooses for his absolution is through death.

The attitude of Sierva Maria and Cayetano towards disease is more or less the same though their reasons and aim are different. They both wholeheartedly accept disease and submit to it wilfully.

Through disease, they seek an escape from the torment imposed upon them. Sierva Maria's torment was thrust upon her by her father, the society and religion, while Cayetano's torment was self inflicted. Finally, for the onlookers, a disease is a ground for stigma and isolation. The lack of empathy must be considered a reason for this. Unless the person himself or herself is not affected by a disease, he/she is unable to feel the difficulty of the person. The way they express their sympathy too is not out of compassion but due to pity.

The General in his Labyrinth is written as an outsider looking in with flashbacks to explicit occasions in the life of Simon Bolivar, "the General". The General is getting ready for his excursion towards the port of Cartagena de Indias, aiming to leave Colombia for Europe. The General leaves Bogota with the couple of authorities still dedicated to him, including his compatriot and confidant, Jose Palacios. After many postponements, the General and his party show up in Honda, where the Governor, Posada Gutierrez, has sorted out for three days of holidays.

The gathering stays a night in Puerto Real, where the General cases he sees a lady singing during the evening. His confidants and the security personnel direct a pursuit, however they were unable to reveal any indication of a lady having been nearby. The General and his company show up at the port of Mompox. Following a few days, the General and his company set out for Turbaco, from where it was planned to proceed to Cartagena the next day, however the General is educated that there is no accessible boat headed for Europe from the port that his visa actually has not shown up.

The General at long last accepts his visa, and after two days he sets off with his escort for Cartagena and the coast, where more gatherings are held in his honour. The General is presently told by one of his confidants that General Rafael Urdaneta has assumed control over the public authority in Bogota, and there are reports of showings and uproars on the side of Bolivar's return. He completes his excursion in Santa Marta, too powerless to even consider proceeding and with just his attendant and his nearest associates close by.

The illness of the General was in his own mind. He perceived himself to be a severely sick person. The minor health conditions that he had such as constipation were never life threatening issues. But he felt them to be caused by some serious hidden diseases. Moreover, given his superhuman persona and the status of the great liberator, he found it less of himself to consult doctor. To him, it was weakness of character to fall sick. Till the final few days of his life never consulted doctors for the medical conditions that bothered him. But, by then, he had come to a state of illness which was caused by his psyche. The state of his psyche is visible in his words. "I'm old, sick, tired, disillusioned, harassed, slandered, and unappreciated."(*GHL*, 205)

Conclusion

Illnesses, both mental and physical, are prominent features in the works of Garcia Marquez. Certain diseases featured in the works are astonishingly fascinating and reminiscent of magical realism which is a significant trait of Garcia Marquez's writing. Various aspects of diseases and their impacts on the characters are discussed in this chapter. The features under consideration are illness and society, combating illness, love as an illness, conquering illness through hope and individualism, and illness and psyche.

It is found that the characters in the select works are initially taken aback when they are exposed to strange or new illnesses. But with time they learn to live through and with these diseases as they acquire more knowledge about it. They also learn to conquer these diseases with their hope and individualism. At times, they also make use of these diseases for personal advantage too. Therefore, it is concluded that fear springs from lack of knowledge and once knowledge is acquired the fear could be defeated. Moreover, hope for light at the end of darkness and ability to improvise and adapt could lead one to success.

CHAPTER SIX
CONCLUSION

The detonation of Latin American literature was closely associated with the major writers of the Latin American Boom. Carlos Fuentes, Julio Cortazar, Mario Vargas Llosa, and Gabriel Garcia Marquez published their books in the Boom era of the 1960s. Critics continued to publish important and useful studies in which writers ranked by their date of birth, but novelists themselves were participating in a continental upheaval that affected equally younger and older writers; and thereby a crisis centred on the Cuban Revolution that became known as Boom. While only few novelists became identified with the Boom as well as others later, there are many other writes that merit attention, occupied in the mapping of the rapidly changing national reality or in surrealist, existentialist, feminist, or other projects. When the linguistic sophistication reaches a new height and novelists turned more to a reflection on their own writings; a fiction or metafiction of a postmodern society, where all is equally significant.

Gabriel Garcia Marquez is an internationally renowned figure in the history of Latin American literature. Readers as well as critics praised him for the magic of the ultimate genre he followed throughout his literary career masked under magical realism. The novel *One Hundred Years of Solitude* was an enigma of his writings. It is the saga of Colonel Aurelino Buendia's Family. Garcia Marquez narrates the fable from primitivism to Modernism. His writing proves that the social and aristocratic lifestyle had solitude. Every character suffers from the solitude in the novel. It is the definite theme in his writings, which is also seen in his other works like, *Love in the Time of Cholera, The General in His Labyrinth, No One Writes to the Colonel* and *Of Love and Other Demons.*

The reputation of Garcia Marquez's writing earned him friendship with Fidel Castro, the former President of Cuba. In a 1982 interview, Garcia Marquez spoke about this friendship to Claudia Dreifus: "Ours is an intellectual friendship. It may not be widely known that Fidel is a very cultured man". Castro says without any pause, that Gabo is his best friend. In the writings of Garcia Marquez, solitude or melancholy was the foremost element. The speech he delivered at the time of the Nobel prize is the best on "Solitude of Latin America". Though winning the prize brought him fame and fortune, his political activism is well known, and his newspaper columns, as well as his essays, short stories and novels, often reflect his political interest in fighting for egalitarian goals.

Marquez's novels reflect the Latin American scenario. We see the conflict between the past and present as the characters in his fiction struggle with the problems of technological change and the industrial revolution. His individual characters are often idiosyncratic figures who manifest a certain solitude which is characteristic of the New World. His books thus depict the reality of Latin America sometimes taking help of magic and sometimes myth, for example *One Hundred Years of Solitude* can be said to be the third world's view point of history rather than the American view. His novels also demonstrate the dynamics of cyclical renewal and contradict the concept of linear progress dominant in the western world and inherent to the traditional concept of America. His books can be related to cultural history and ideology. Marquez in an essay 'Latin American Impossible Reality' says.

> "*We, writers from Latin American and the Caribbean have to confess, with our hands over our heart, that reality is a better writer than we are, ourdestiny, and perhaps our glory, is to try and imitate it with humility, to the best of our ability. (1985)*"

Marquez can be distinguished from the writers of the old world in his innovation in the structure of the novel. He experiments with narrative techniques within the form of the novel. Marquez himself plays an important role in his novels as the narrator. He narrates in a matter-of-fact tone passing no judgement on his characters. He intermingles with the crowd in his novels. In *One Hundred Years of Solitude* he is a minor character, while in *the Autumn of the Patriarch*, the narrator is referred to as "we" but in spite of his being an omniscient narrator he is conscious of the conflict brewing between the story he narrates and the time taken to narrate it for instance, in *The Autumn of the Patriarch*. There is hardly any punctuation, so the novel gives an appearance of a breathless race against time and energy to complete an endless commentary on the life of a despot.

Marquez's books inquire about the relationship between history and human consciousness as well as raise questions concerning the nature of a reality as burdensome and problematic as that of Latin America. He effectively combines the imaginary and concocted reality and his works are often set in a time and at a location of political turmoil and subjugation, his novels reverberate with political implication. He gives *One Hundred Years of Solitude* a political interpretation by saying that it is a metaphor for Latin America. Marquez has debated the culture, history and politics of Latin America. The concepts of violence, love and culture are debated in *Love in the Time of Cholera* through the characters living in a small Caribbean town at the beginning of the twentieth century.

In his books the themes of incest, sex, fate, destiny, personal identity, dreams, memory, nostalgia, deconstruction and reconstruction of history, cyclic and linear time, death and life are intricately interwoven into the main three leitmotifs of love, power and solitude. Thus a unique Marquezian vision emerges substantiating his preoccupation with the controversial aspect of human experience. Martin aptly says:

"*Garcia Marquez is a rare instance of the sort of writer often daydreamed about by modern booklovers and literati - an artistically serious, technically and intellectually sophisticated, politically progressive author whose works enjoy popular acclaim. (1988)*"

Garcia Marquez is widely regarded as one of the most representative writers of Latin America, as well as someone who has a perfect understanding of the pulse of the continent. The immense socio-political abnormalities, historical heritage, and ethnic diversities that characterise Latin America find a home in Garcia Marquez's fictions.

As Gerald Martin says, "the continent's characteristic and persistent alternation between utopia and apocalypse, euphoria and black desp lir" (ibid) is best embodied in his works.

Garcia Marquez and His Style

His political views are not entirely clear; some claim that he is a supporter of communism, but some disagree. Growing up, his grandparents had the greatest impact on his life. While his grandfather was a liberal political leader in the town who influenced him with his political philosophy, his grandmother was a superstitious woman who told Garcia Marquez stories based on fantastic myths that were told in his hometown. In later years, Garcia Marquez would credit her with being the inspiration for his storytelling style, which he would come to call magical realism. General Gustavo Rojas Pinilla's regime would go on to slaughter a large number of Colombians during this period, including Gaitan, the leader of the Liberal party in the country. It was 1955 when Garcia Marquez left Colombia. Prensa Latina, the Cuban news agency, hired him as a staff writer and photographer. As a result of his friendship with Castro, the communist leader, he is widely regarded as a staunch communist believer.

Although this relationship is not indicative of Garcia Marquez's political views, he did spend part of the 1970s working on a novel about the flaws of Castro's regime and life in Cuba, which was published in 1978. He then relocated to Mexico City, where he continued his journalism career while also honing his novel-writing abilities; he achieved fame with the publication of *One Hundred Years of Solitude* in 1967, which was the first novel written by Garcia Marquez in English. The radical liberal views of Marquez's grandfather, as well as military dictators like General Pinilla during the 1950s, were particularly influential on his writings and life. The dictator General Pinilla and imperialists such as those in the United States do not deserve to be the victims of Latin American countries' own development, according to him.

The literary and commercial profusion thus produced works that were exciting, creative, innovative, imaginative and that proposed theoretical issues pertaining to reading, writing, spoken language, translation, history and fiction. These are significant when we realize that the Latin American reality was not conducive to writers and their works. In fact Mario Vargas Llosa says that, "The historical reality, the framework of experience within which the Latin American novelist writes, is a reality threatened with extinction". (1977)

A socio-political heritage that was incongruous and lawless was passed down to Latin America, and this heritage was farther bastardized and despoiled by the many but important coven that governed the recently autonomous countries. The struggle for dominance and rule redounded in a slew of civil wars and revolutions, which crowned in political, profitable, and social complaint, chaos, and confusion, which eventually led to the junction of utmost countries under dictatorial administrations. Authoritarian administrations and cathartic military totalitarianism have been an necessary and habitual point of the political geography in Latin America. Politics in Colombia has been embrangle down in a bitter haul- of- war between the country's two major political parties, the rightists and the Liberals. The contest between them, which has been fuelled by ideological differences, has been the root cause of multitudinous civil wars and internal strife throughout history.

The in-depth examination of Marquez's life and career demonstrates how intricately his inventions are intertwined with his particular gests. Because he was the grandson of a colonel, Marquez was formerly being tutored in political matters, and as a young boy, he was formerly apprehensive of the corruption in the state, having witnessed his forefather stay for his war pension for an interminable period of time, which did not arrive.

However, it was Gaitan's murder in broad daylight on the streets of Bogata in 1948 that provided him with his first real life experience. Within an hour, the city of Bogota was engulfed in flames, effectively putting an end to Marquez's studies there. Colombia remained under siege for more than a decade after that, with the military repressing any anti-government authority and strict censorship imposed on newspapers and other media outlets alike.

Garcia Marquez has not written a complete novel about La Violencia but there are traces of it in his fiction. He is writing about the society which is full of oppression, killing, murder, chaos, uncertainty. People are being killed openly, Garcia Marquez is writing about trauma, which has been faced by the living and not by the dead. As discussed above violence has its roots in colonial Colombia and it continues to be there also after decolonization. So it is obvious that the novels of Marquez are prevalent with the atmosphere of violence, which has deep impact on the psyche and sensibility of the common people. The only two political parties of Colombia wanted to remain in power at any cost, if so people will be happy or sad.

A Critique of the Selected Works

The story of Bolivar is told in *The General in His Labyrinth,* and Garcia Marquez attempts to delve deeply into the mechanisms of power once more through this narrative. The various political battles, as well as the chaos and instability that have resulted in the rise of a desire for power. As a warrior and administrator, Bolivar is the first iconic, historical figure of a powerful hero, whose fame and glory are inextricably linked to his exploits as a warrior and administrator. The never-ending wars, conspiracies, power struggles, and so on create a maze of confusion from which Bolivar finds it difficult to find his way back out. When it comes to Latin American politics and life, the term and concept of labyrinth is well-known. This is because conquests and peace treaties are often followed by wars and bloodshed, and this cycle continues indefinitely, creating a vicious circle.

The brilliance of *No One Writes to the Colonel* stands out when it is contrasted with the many novels of social protest written in Spanish America during the same period, which were heavy-handed, with a profuse rhetoric. Like the other works of Garcia Marquez, this work too features real life incidents and characters. The protagonist of the novella, the Colonel is strikingly similar to his maternal grandfather Colonel Nicholas. The story of the Colonel's wait for his pension is a depiction of the plight of Colonel Nicholas, a veteran of the Thousand Days' War, who waited for his pension cheques throughout his life time.

Through *One Hundred Years of Solitude*, Garcia Marquez has widened his perspectives so that he could depict the biases and issue of the whole landmass of South America. A serious reworking of the historical backdrop of the mainland, hundred years long the narrative of Macondo's is likewise a parodic disruption of the standard European (as well as North American; domineering disposition and viewpoint towards the landmass).

Garcia Marquez spoofs and mocks essentially every part of Spanish imperialism in Latin America, as well as thinking about the ongoing political circumstance in the nation. A humorous reflection on a previous history produced through savage severity and viciousness that fills in as a cloak for a frightening present reality of rebellion and tyranny, the unending nationwide conflicts, fights for control, financial reliance, and so on, are undeniably portrayed in the book.

Love in the Time of Cholera is a typical saga of love persevering through a time of adversity. The novel portrays the difficult times through which a country travelled, that also became the backdrop for a couple to seek out the best moments of their life and experience the fever of first love. This novel also discusses various interpretations of love. The devastating effects of the cholera epidemic and the social inequality prevalent in Latin American society find representation in the novel. It further lashes out at the civic administration of the country which does nothing for the downtrodden.

Of Love and Other Demons is an all-out attack on religious authorities in a postcolonial context. The demonization, isolation, physical torture and finally tragic death of Sierva Maria depicted in the novel serves as a moral for all those who tend to disregard authorities. Moral corruption of the clergy is also featured in the novel. Furthermore, a politically incorrect version of love which leads to statutory rape finds place in this novel.

Major Findings of the Study

This book is an attempt to understand the psychological elements featured deep inside the select works of Garcia Marquez. Two major theories have been used to analyse the themes of individualism, hope and illness portrayed in the selected works. The study also tries to understand the working mechanism of the characters' minds and, in-turn formulates strategies to face and overcome similar situations in real life. The observations made in this thesis are mainly four.

The third chapter of this thesis has taken the topic of individualism as its focal point. To a certain extent, individualism features as a personal trait in all the major characters of Garcia Marquez's works. Various aspects of individualism such as individualism and society, competitive individualism, methodological individualism, and individualism in love and relationship, those are visible in these works are analysed using Leon Festinger's Cognitive Dissonance Theory. A deep analysis of the circumstances and logical results relationship of the individualism exhibited by the characters and their outcomes, one might say that specific characters are effective in their endeavour while others come up short or die. This leads to the initial observation that most characters are highly individualistic.

They never lose their personality and character. The results of these are not always positive. Some of them end up unsuccessful or dead. Thus, it could be inferred that individualism is a double edged sword. It must be wielded carefully. Individualistic behaviour is highly emotional. Hence, it could be used to set goals in life but the path towards it should be logical and rational.

Chapter IV focuses on various aspects of hope and how it impacts a particular character. The aspects such as self-motivation through hope, hope in love and relationship, losing hope and failing, suffering in hope, and hope and psyche are analysed with the help of C.R. Snyder's Hope Theory. The study has found that most characters in these works are highly hopeful in their lives. While some of them put in serious effort to achieve the objectives with a positive feeling of the possibility of succeeding, other characters mere hope and lie in wait of their desires coming true. The first group of characters end up succeed in their mission whereas the latter group suffer failure or even worse lose their lives.

Therefore, the second observation is that most characters are driven by hope.

Some characters take action to achieve their hope while others hope in vain and ultimately lose hope. Those who take action emerge victorious while others perish. From this, it could be inferred that hope can be a highly motivating factor. Without hope, no one can achieve anything. But, mere hope cannot lead one to success, it requires strenuous effort too.

In Chapter V which deals with illness as its central theme, it is seen that the characters in the select works are at first shocked when they are presented to peculiar or new diseases. Be that as it may, with time they figure out how to survive and with these infections as they secure more information about it. They additionally figure out how to vanquish these sicknesses with their expectation and independence. On occasion, they likewise utilize these sicknesses for individual benefit as well. Accordingly, it is reasoned that dread springs from absence of information and whenever information is gained the trepidation could be crushed. In addition, trust for light toward the finish of murkiness and capacity to make do and adjust could lead one to progress.

Hence, the third observation is that when coming face to face with a disease, all the characters are taken aback in panic. But, once they understand more about the same, they learn to tame it and even use it to their benefit. The inference drawn is that the fear and panic springs from ignorance of the situation. Once it is deeply analysed and understood, it could be used for one's benefit.

Finally, it is observed that the characters do not give in to societal pressure and end up living happily on their own terms, though they may not have achieved material success. It is thus inferred that happiness and contentment in life may be achieved not only through material success or wealth but also through following one's own ideals and deep desires.

To conclude, the thesis statement can be recapitulated as objective oriented individualism devoid of obsession can lead one to a life of contentment, and hope coupled with tireless effort is the fuel to move forward in life.

Quintet Postulates

A set of postulates that could be helpful to achieve contentment in life is being surmised here. They are titled Quintet Postulates. They are –

1. Let emotion determine your destination, and logic, its path.

While choosing a career path or pursuit in life, it is always better to fix the goal based on emotional thinking as the attainment of the goal has to appeal to the emotion. Goals selected through logical thinking may offer material success but may make the person regret missing all the interesting and light hearted moments in life. The goal which is decided upon through emotional thinking could help the individual to understand the true value of it. At the same time the path towards the goal should be selected based on logic. Thus, the person would be able to attain the goal easily and not set any irrational goal.

2. Let not emotion overrule logic and vice-versa.

While in the pursuit of life one should never lose the balance between emotion and logic. Emotions and logic should go hand in hand so that either are not compromised and in turn, create a harmony between mind and brain. This keeps the individual grounded and prevents regret in future life. Equal priority should be given to emotion and logic to yield optimum results.

3. Let your hope be backed by your effort.

Hope should always be backed up by serious effort. One cannot merely hope to attain a goal and be successful in achieving it. The individual should put in serious effort to achieve the goal and the motivation to put in effort can be derived from the hope of achieving the goal.

4. Know the difference between an objective and an obsession.

One should always know the difference between an objective and an obsession. An objective is an achievable and realistic goal that is decided upon by an individual after weighing the pros and cons, while an obsession is an unrealistic and potentially harmful mental desire to achieve or possess something. Thus, one should be careful in distinguishing an obsession from an objective and pursue only realistic objectives. Else, the individual is bound to cause harm to themselves or any other individual involved.

5. Fear not the unknown, analyse it, understand it and leverage it.

People generally fear unknown or relative new ideas and things out of suspicion of potential danger. To a certain extent, this fear keeps people safe. But, fear is also an obstacle that prevents people from venturing into new fields and ideas. So, one should not let the lack of knowledge towards a certain idea to cause a fear towards it in their mind. Through careful analysis and keen observation, one could learn more about the alien ideas and overcome the fear. Further, one learns to utilise the idea or thing after gaining knowledge about it.

Recommendations for Future Research

Recommendations for future research on Garcia Marquez's works are as follows:

- The findings of this study may be applied in experimental psychological studies to formulate practical solutions for the problems.
- Studies can be done to analyse the pessimistic attitude of the characters.
- The female characters could be studied under a feministic perspective to understand their moral foibles and the accuracy in their characterisation.
- Elements of Marxism and impact of the author's political ideology can be studied.
- Studies can be done on the postmodern aspects in the works of Garcia Marquez.
- The influence of war, politics and religion on women may also be studied.
- Comparative studies can be done on the social milieus of Garcia Marquez and other authors.
- Studies can be done to uncover the recapitulation of personal history in Garcia Marquez's works.
- Politics of love and sex can be studied to understand the new meanings and relation between these terms.
- Rewriting of History in the post-truth era.

Select Bibliography

Primary Sources

Primary Sources

Garcia Marquez, Gabriel. *Love in the Time of Cholera*. New York: Alfred A. Knopf. 1988. Print.

---. *No One Writes to the Colonel*. New York: Harper & Row. 1979. Print.

---. *Of Love and Other Demons*. New York: Penguin Books. 1996. Print.

---. *One Hundred Years of Solitude*. New York: Harper Perennial Modern Classics. 2006. Print.

---. *The General in His Labyrinth*. New York: A.A. Knopf. 1990. Print.

Secondary Sources

Anderson, Jon Lee. "The Power of Gabriel Garcia Marquez". The New Yorker. 27 September 1999. pp. 56-69. Print.

Arnau, Randolph. C et al. A Spanish language version of the Herth Hope Scale : Development and Psychometric Evaluation in a Peruvial Sample. Educational and Psychological Measurement. Vol. 17, No. 5. 2010. pp. 808-824. Print.

Bell, M. "Gabriel García Marquez". *Modern Novelists*. London, Palgrave. 1993. Print.

Bell-Villada, Gene H., *Gabriel Garcia Marquez: the Man and his Work*. University of California Press. 1990. Print.

Bloom, Harold. Ed. *Modern Critical Views: Gabriel Garcia Marquez*. New York: Chelsea House Publishers. 1989. Print.

Booker, M. Keith. "The Dangers of Gullible Reading: Narrative as Seduction in Garcia Marquez's *Love in the Time of Cholera*." Studies in Twentieth Century Literature. 17.2. 1993. pp. 181-195. Print.

Brody, Robert. Mario Vargas Llosa and the Totalisation Impulse. Texas Studies in Literature and Language, Vol. 19, No.4. 1977. pp. 514-521. Print.

Buehrer, David. "A Second Chance on Earth: The Postmodern and the Post-Apocalyptic in Garcia Marquez's *Love in the Time of Cholera.*" 1990. Print.

Castronovo, David. "*Love in the Time of Cholera*". America. 10 September, 1988. pp. 146-8. Print.

Couteau, Robert. "*Love in the Time of Cholera*". Arete Magazine. December 1988. http://members.tripod.com/more_couteau/marquez.htm. 20 December 2021. Web.

Clemmons, Walter. "The Sweet Plague of Love." Newsweek, 25 April 1988. pp. 60-61. Print. Fahy, Tom. Gabriel Garcia Marquez's *Love in the Time of Cholera*. 2003. Print.

Fiddian, Robin. "A Prospctive Post-Script: Apropos of *Love in the Time of Cholera.*" *Gabriel Garcia Marquez: New Readings*. 1987. pp. 191-205. Print.

Garcia Marquez, Gabriel. "The Solitude of Latin America." *Gabriel Garcia Marquez: New Readings*. 1987. pp. 207-11. Print.

Hamill, Pete. "Love and Solitude." Vanity Fair, March 1988.pp. 124-31. Print.

Jones A.H. Literature and Medicine: García Márquez' Love in the Time of Cholera.

In: Butler R.N., Jasmin C. (eds) Longevity and Quality of Life. Boston, Springer. 2000. MA. https://doi.org/10.1007/978-1-4615-4249-0_36. 12 January, 2022. Web.

Martin, Gerald. *Journeys through the Labyrinth*. London: Verso. 1989. Print.

Martinez-Maldonado, Manuel. "Numbers, Death, and Time in Garcia Marquez's *Love in the Time of Cholera*". *The Body and the Text: Comparative Essays in Literature and Medicine*. Eds. Bruce Clarke and Wendell Aycock. Lubbock: Texas Tech University Press. 1990. pp. 127-37. Print.

McGuirk, Bernard and Richard Cardwell, Eds. *Gabriel Garcia Marquez: New Readings*.

Cambridge, Mass: Cambridge University Press. 1987. Print.

McHale, Brian. *Postmodernist Fiction*. New York: Routledge. 1987. Print.

McMurray, George R. (ed.), *CriticalEssaysonGabrielGarciaMarquez*. Boston: Hall. 1987. Print.

Millington, Mark. I. *GarciaMarquez'sNovelsofLove*. Ed. Philip Swanson, *TheCambridge Companion to Gabriel Garcia Marquez*. Cambridge University Press. 2010. Print.

Minta, Stephen, *Gabriel Garcia Marquez: Writer of Columbia*. Icon. 1987. Print. Morana, Mabel. "Modernity and Marginality in *Love in the Time of Cholera*". Studies in Twentieth Century Literature, 14.1. 1990. pp. 27-43. Print.

---"The Novel as Tropical Flower". The Economist, 2 July 1988. pp. 77-78. Print. Ortega, Julio (ed.), *Gabriel Garcia Marquez and the Powers of Fiction*. Austin: University of Texas Press, 1988. Print.

Penuel, Arnold M. *Intertextuality in Garcia Marquez*. South Carolina: Spanish Literature Publications Company. 1994. Print.

Ramachandran, Sreejith and K, Rajkumar. Re-writing History in Gabriel Garcia Marquez's *Of Love and Other Demons*. International Journal of English Language and Literature in Humanities, Vol. 7, 2019, pp. 1867-1875. Print.

---. Hope and Despair in the Select Works of Gabriel Garcia Marquez. International Journal of Humanities and Social Science Invention, Vol. 9, 2020, pp. 38-40. Print.

---. Elements of Postcolonialism in Gabriel Garcia Marquez's *One Hundred Years of Solitude* and *Love in the Time of Cholera*. Bodhi International Journal of Research in Humanities, Arts and Science, Vol. 4, 2020, pp. 13-17. Print.

---. A Stylistic Study of the Select Novels of Gabriel Garcia Marquez. Journal of Interdisciplinary Cycle Research, Vol. XII, No. XI, 2020. Print.

---. The Portrayal of Diseases in the Select Works of Gabriel Garcia Marquez. IOSR Journal of Humanities and Social Science (IOSR-JHSS), Vol. 26, No. 3, Series 6, 2021, pp. 38-40. Print.

---. Individualism as a Way of Life in the Select Works of Gabriel Garcia Marquez. Journal of Interdisciplinary Cycle Research, Vol. XIII, No. VIII, 2021. Print.

Rorty, Richard. *Philosophy and Social Hope*: Penguin. 2000. Print.

Sims, Robert L., *The Evolution of Myth in Gabriel Garcia Marquez*. Miami: Ediciones Universal. 1981. Print.

Snyder, C.R. *Psychology of Hope: You can get Here from There.* Free Press. 2010. Print.

Wood, Michael, *Gabriel Garcia Marquez: One Hundred Yean of Solitude*. Cambridge University Press. 1990. Print.

Zamora, Lois Parkinson, and Wendy B Faris. Eds. *Magical Realism: Theory, History, Community*. Durham: Duke University Press. 1995. Print.

Other Sources

Booth, Wayne C. et al. *The Craft of Research,* University of Chicago. 2008. Print. Brause, Rita S. *Writing Your Doctoral Dissertation: Invisible Rules for Success*, Routledge. 2000. Print.

Bryant, Miles T. *The Portable Dissertation Advisor.* Sage. 2003. Print.

Calabrese, Raymond L. *Dissertation Desk Reference: the Doctoral Student's Manual to Writing the Dissertation.* Rowman and Little Field Education. 2009. Print.

Clark, Irene L. *Writing the Successful Thesis and Dissertation.* Prentice Hall. 2007. Print.

Feak, Christine B. and Swales John M. *Telling a Research Story: Writing a Literature Review*. Michigan Press. 2009. Print.

Fink, Arlene. *Conducting Research Literature Reviews.* Sage. 2009. Print.

Galvan, Jose L. *Writing Literature Reviews: A Guide for Students of the Social and Behavioral Sciences.* Taylor and Francis Ltd. 2009. Print.

Hart, Christopher. *Doing a Literature Review: Releasing the Social Science Research Imagination*. Sage. 1999. Print.

https://www.mentalhelp.net/poc/view-doc.php- "Mental Health, Depression, Anxiety, Wellness, Family & Relationship Issues, Sexual Disorders & ADHD Medications", 12 January, 2020. Web.

http://icpla.edu/wpcontent/uploads/2012/10/winnicott-D-The-Antisocial-Tendency.pdf/.27 August, 2019. Web.

Jesson, Jill. et al. *Doing Your Literature Review: Traditional and Systematic Techniques*. Sage. 2011. Print.

Kothari, C.R. and Garg Gaurav. *Research Methodology: Methods and Techniques*. New Age International Publishers. 2019. Print.

Luey, Beth. *Revising Your Dissertation - Advice from Leading Editors*. Free Press. 2004. Print.

Machi, Lawrence Anthony and McEvoy, Brenda T. *The Literature Review: Six Steps to Success*. Sage. 2008. Print.

MLA. *MLA Handbook for Writers of Research Papers*. Affiliated East-West Press Pvt.Ltd. 2008. Print.

Pan, M. Ling. *Preparing Literature Reviews: Qualitative and Quantitative Approaches*. Routledge. 2004. Print.

Ridley, Diana. *The Literature Review-A Step-by-Step Guide for Students*. Sage. 2008. Print.

Roberts, Carol M. *The Dissertation Journey*. Sage. 2004. Print.

Single, Peg Boyle. *Demystifying Dissertation Writing*. Stylus. 2009. Print.

Swetnam, Derek. *Writing Your Dissertation: How to Plan, Prepare and Present your Work Successfully*. How to Books. 1997. Print.

www.ingramcontent.com/pod-product-compliance
Lightning Source LLC
LaVergne TN
LVHW021139160826
845679LV00023B/1967

9798894461656